Faith Steps FOR **MILITARY FAMILIES**

Faith Steps
FOR
MILITARY FAMILIES

Spiritual Readiness Through the Psalms of Ascent

LISA NIXON PHILLIPS

NEW YORK

Faith Steps FOR **MILITARY FAMILIES**
Spiritual Readiness Through the Psalms of Ascent

Published in New York, New York, by Morgan James Publishing. Morgan James and The Entrepreneurial Publisher are trademarks of Morgan James, LLC.
www.MorganJamesPublishing.com

The Morgan James Speakers Group can bring authors to your live event. For more information or to book an event visit The Morgan James Speakers Group at www.TheMorganJamesSpeakersGroup.com.

Unless otherwise indicated, all Scripture quotations are from the New Revised Standard Version of the Bible, copyright ©) 1989 by World Bible Publishers, Inc. Used by permission. All rights reserved.

Verses marked NKJV are taken from the New King James Version. Copyright © 1982 by Thomas Nelson, Inc. Used by permission. All rights reserved.

Verses marked NLT are taken from the Holy Bible, New Living Translation, copyright © 1996, 1004. Used by permission of Tyndale House Publishers, Inc., Wheaton, IL. 60189 USA. All rights reserved.

Verses marked MSG are taken from *The Message*. Copyright © by Eugene H. Peterson 1993, 1994, 1995, 1996, 2000, 2001, 2002. Used by permission of NavPress Publishing Group.

FREE eBook edition for your existing eReader with purchase

PRINT NAME ABOVE

For more information, instructions, restrictions, and to register your copy, go to **www.bitlit.ca/readers/register** or use your QR Reader to scan the barcode:

ISBN 978-1-61448-996-2 paperback
ISBN 978-1-61448-997-9 eBook
ISBN 978-1-61448-999-3 hardcover
Library of Congress Control Number:
2013952872

Cover Design by:
Rachel Lopez
www.r2cdesign.com

Interior Design by:
Bonnie Bushman
bonnie@caboodlegraphics.com

In an effort to support local communities, raise awareness and funds, Morgan James Publishing donates a percentage of all book sales for the life of each book to Habitat for Humanity Peninsula and Greater Williamsburg.

Get involved today, visit
www.MorganJamesBuilds.com.

Habitat for Humanity®
Peninsula and
Greater Williamsburg
Building Partner

TABLE OF CONTENTS

ACKNOWLEDGEMENTS

I wish to thank several people for making this book possible. At Morgan James Publishing, I want to thank Terry Whalin, acquisitions editor, for believing in my book topic, the Entrepreneur Vision Mastermind team: David Hancock, Jim Howard, and Rick Frishman. Thank you for recognizing the need for spiritual readiness in our military families. I also thank Margo Toulouse, my author relations manager and those who work with her at Morgan James for walking me through the publication process and answering my many questions. Thank you all for giving me this opportunity to see this book come to fruition.

My husband, Ray, a retired machinist mate chief in the U.S. Navy: I'm so grateful for your support and cheering me on in this new journey, and giving me the time and space to write for hours on end. Thank you, dear, for caring so deeply for me and my call to writing.

My daughter, Megan, a first lieutenant in the Army National Guard: Thank you for your willingness to come and work in the family business so I could be home writing. Thank you for your gift of time. I'm so proud of your military accomplishments. You've become one strong and resilient army girl and this mother couldn't be prouder. And for my son-in-law, Josh, I'm appreciative of your support and pride in Megan's military commitment.

My son, Lawrence, who stepped up his help around the house, putting up with many lame dinners because I was buried in my manuscript: You're a remarkable son. I look forward to seeing if God leads you to a career in the military, following in your father's and sister's footsteps.

My father, Alan Nixon: Thank you for your loving and personal words of support. They mean the world to me. I pray this book will magnify your faith.

My mothers-in-law Marilyn Phillips and Mary Bergenholtz: Thank you for your interest and support of my book. I hope as you read it, you'll be blessed and your faith refreshed.

Donna Clark Goodrich: Thank you for adding me to your busy work and writing schedule to do the editing of my book. I appreciate you for all the help along the way. I would have been lost without your guidance. And I'm honored to have you as a new friend.

My fellow writer friend Kathy Opie: Thank you for being that dear friend who supported me and my children through ship deployments. Your gift of hospitality and your many cards of encouragement when the military life became hard were such a blessing.

Beverly Beattie and her late husband, Gene: Thank you for being "our family across the street" helping me with everything from car issues to broken garage doors–from watching my children so I could pursue my accounting degree to having us over for dinners. Thank you for your loving hospitality and dear friendship.

My dear Kansas friend for over 30 years, Jeannie Furst: Thank you for encouraging me to keep at the writing craft. Your belief in me, your prayers for me, and your words of affirmation have blessed me immensely.

And my greatest thanks to my Lord and Savior Jesus for teaching me many spiritual lessons–good and loving ones, challenging and painful ones, and those still to come to be used for writing for Him.

INTRODUCTION

FAITH MAKES A DIFFERENCE

In Leviticus 23 God ordained seven national celebrations called "festivals" for the Israelites to observe. His purpose for these festivals was to establish worship and fellowship into Israel's culture, and He commanded the Israelites to designate a time of coming together for spiritual renewal and thanksgiving for all God had accomplished on their behalf.

There were three festivals that required them to travel to Jerusalem: Passover, Pentecost, and the Festival of Tabernacles. It is here that the Psalms of Ascent come into play. They are a group of fifteen hymns from Psalms 120-134 which the Israelites (also referred to as pilgrims) would sing as they made the difficult journey by foot to Jerusalem. Written by various authors—including king's Hezekiah, David, and Solomon—each psalm communicates a theme or a concern common in their day. Behind such themes as fear, danger, hostility protection, trust, contentment, joy, sorrow, harassment, and honor are genuine accounts of real people who experienced life in raw form. They're honest testimonies sung with deep emotion. Centuries old, yet the topics in the Psalms of Ascent are of great concern or interest to military service members and their families today. Tucked within the themes are rich and distinctive metaphors, which expand our understanding of the psalms and amplifies their relevance to the culture and faith of the ancient Israelites. As the pilgrims traveled, they recited the psalms, each one a step in their trek to Jerusalem. The overarching premise of the Psalms of Ascent is that their faith in God made a significant difference in the outcome of their lives.

The psalms are timely in light of America's recent war campaigns. Military families can draw vital spiritual lessons that can contribute to their spiritual readiness levels as they answer the call of their commander-in-chief to support and defend America's moral values, its Judeo-Christian faith and her freedoms.

The title "Psalms of Ascent" originated from several suggested meanings. The most widely known one is that the fifteen psalms relate to the fifteen steps going from the Court of Women to the Court of Israel in the temple in Jerusalem. (If you have a study Bible, check in the Topical Index for "temple" to see if a temple diagram is provided.) Another suggested view is the relationship between Mount Zion and the location of the temple in Jerusalem. Seemingly, the pilgrims continued to sing these psalms as they ascended Mount Zion to reach the temple. It is also worth noting that because these psalms were sung, they're also referred to as the *"Songs of Ascent"* and also as the *"Pilgrim's Songs."*

I've also seen the Psalms of Ascent referred to as "**Songs of Degrees**," a view presented by John Lightfoot and E. Thirtle.[1] This view makes a correlation between King Hezekiah and the degrees on his father's, King Ahaz's, sundial. Sundials in this period were sometimes made in the form of miniature staircases so that the shadows moved up and down the steps.[2] Second Kings 20 gives the story of Hezekiah's brush with death. Because he came down ill and wasn't expected to recover, the prophet Isaiah told him to put his affairs in order. In great distress, Hezekiah prayed to God, calling attention to his faithfulness to Him as a king (v. 3). Moved by the king's prayer, God healed him and gave the king an additional fifteen years of life. Because there was some doubt on the part of the king that God would do as He promised, the king asked for a sign.[3] Isaiah told Hezekiah that God would turn the shadow on the steps back by ten degrees. "The prophet Isaiah cried to the LORD; and he brought the shadow back the ten intervals, by which the sun had declined on the dial of Ahaz" (v. 11). Because there are ten Psalms of Ascent in which the authors are not identified, the suggestion is they were written by King Hezekiah matching the ten degrees that the sundial retreated,[4] with the remaining five authored by the others already mentioned. In 2 Kings 20:5 is an interesting association. God instructed King Hezekiah, upon his healing to *go up* to the temple on the third day.[5]

Some authors group the Psalms of Ascent by topic. For example, Psalm 127 and 128 deal with the home and family and therefore are placed next to each other. The same applies to Psalm 130, which praises God for His grace and forgiveness, with Psalm 131 focusing on an attitude of humility, the appropriate response towards such a priceless gift. My presentation of the Psalms of Ascent in this book reflect commonly held views for a practical approach for understanding and applying the spiritual principles of each psalm to experiences common to the military lifestyle.

For the greatest benefit, read the Psalm of Ascent that precedes each chapter and contemplate the significance of its meaning, considering tone and emotion. Also consider what application the psalm would serve for your life and circumstances now. If you're comfortable with writing in your Bible, consider keeping it next to you when reading each chapter, making notes in the margins.

Have you always wanted to know more about the lives of the ancient Israelites, their culture, faith, trials, triumphs, traditions, and also learn about God's nature in ways that will lead to a deeper worship experience? It is my hope that as you take this journey with me through the Psalms of Ascent, you will find new aspects of God's nature and biblical truths to build resiliency and spiritual readiness into your military marriage, family, and personal journey of faith.

May God bless you from Zion.

Lisa

PSALM OF ASCENT 120

[1] In my distress I cry to the LORD,
    that he may answer me:
[2] "Deliver me, O LORD,
    from lying lips,
    from a deceitful tongue."
[3] What shall be given to you?
    And what more shall be done to you,
    you deceitful tongue?
[4] A warrior's sharp arrows,
    with glowing coals of the broom tree!
[5] Woe is me, that I am an alien in Meshech,
    that I must live among the tents of Kedar.
[6] Too long have I had my dwelling among
    those
    who hate peace.
[7] I am for peace;
    but when I speak,
    they are for war.

★ ★ ★ CHAPTER ONE ★ ★ ★

TROUBLE DURING THE JOURNEY

In my distress I cry to the LORD, that he may answer me.
Psalm 120

In January of 1979, I boarded a plane at the San Francisco
International Airport bound for Kansas City following a week-
long visit with my dad that included a couple of days of snow
skiing. My dad was an airline mechanic for Trans World Airlines
(TWA), so our family traveled often. Flying became an even bigger
part of my life after my parents divorced when I was ten. My mother
took my older brother, Michael, and me back to Lawrence, Kansas,
our home town and where our grandparents on both sides lived.
From then on flying between Kansas and California became routine.
By the time I was seventeen my dad had also taken me to many other
parts of the world.

3

On this particular flight, everything had started out normal enough. Even though I wasn't thrilled at returning home, I was excited as any seventeen-year-old would be about seeing my friends. Because I flew this flight path often, I became familiar with the Rocky Mountains of Colorado. I knew them by sight from my window airplane seat. So, it seemed a bit odd to me that the plane was flying extremely low over the Rockies when we had another hour and a half before landing in Kansas City. My intuition was soon confirmed by the captain when he announced to the passengers that someone back in San Francisco reported placing a bomb aboard this flight. Immediately the flight plan was changed in order to make an emergency landing at the Denver International Airport.

In all my experiences with flying, I hadn't encountered anything like this. The possibility that every second could be my last nearly paralyzed me. What had been a quiet flight was now filled with nervous chatter from the other passengers. A desperate need to get off the plane ruptured and overwhelmed me. A deep penetrating fear overtook my thoughts. I could blow up in midair. If there was any comfort to be had, it was in knowing death would be instantaneous. Ensnared on what could be a doomed flight, I left my seat several times and made tearful distress calls to God in the solitude of the airplane's lavatory. To keep composed, I said what verses I could remember of Psalm 23. There, in my seat, I closed my eyes and pictured myself walking with Jesus beside green pastures and still waters, even though evil had presented itself and I was in a dark valley. By the time the runway lights of the Denver airport came into view, the late afternoon sun had given way to the night sky.

TODAY'S PEARL

"But I trust in you, O Lᴏʀᴅ;
I say, 'You are my God.'
My times are in your hand;
deliver me from the hand of
my enemies and persecutors"
(Psalm 31:14-15).

In what seemed like eternity, the wheels of the plane touched the runway and the heaviness I felt started to ease. Soon I felt the safety of the ground beneath my feet. I continued to whisper parts of Scripture to help me to hold it together. The plane at last came to a stop at the end of the runway. The captain hastily gave the emergency directions, which included leaving behind our carry-ons. Like a disturbed herd of sheep, we scurried out the tail end of the plane and down a ladder into the night's winter chill. Airport buses rushed us to the terminal where we were put under heavy guard while bomb sniffing dogs scoured the plane.

Four hours later we were given the all clear signal and allowed to re-board and continue on to Kansas City, never knowing if the bomb threat was real or not.

As a seventeen-year-old, my faith in Jesus turned a corner that day. I no longer thought of Jesus as simply a Savior, thereby securing my place in heaven. No, God had revealed Himself to me in a whole new dimension—that of my Protector and Helper. Not because I was safe, but because when I was in those desperate moments, there was no one else to place my hopes in. All I could do was take God at His Word, trusting that He was with me like His Word promises.

I learned that life can change in a matter of moments. And it was no different for the Israelites as they started on their journey to the temple in Jerusalem for the annual festivals. Our first Psalm of Ascent likewise opens with a

---

KEY POINT #1

There are times in life when all we can do is take God at His Word.

---

distress call to God. "In my distress I called to the LORD, and He answered me" (Psalm 120:1–2). Today, it would sound more like this: "I'm in trouble, God, and I need your help NOW!" We've all been there at one time or another. The Greek word for anguish is *thlipsis* which means *to crush*, *press, compress*, and *squeeze*.[1] Think of anguish as something pressing down with great weight. Psalm 55:4 denotes the degree of the psalmist's anguish when he says, "My heart pounds in my chest. The terror of death assaults me" (NLT).

The journey to Jerusalem was arduous and it meant traveling by foot through unfamiliar and even hostile territory. Some even traveled from other countries. The psalmist opens with a distress call because he realizes he is in the territory of heathen people. In verse 5, he associates his trek with two cities: Meshech and Kedar. Meschech was located north of Israel near the Black Sea and Kedar was a nation located southeast of Israel.[2] The psalmist used them as a metaphor to represent people who were known to be barbarian and confrontational, and were to be avoided at all costs.[3] Here, our psalmist reveals that he feels much like a foreigner.

Have you ever lived or been stationed in a place that was particularly challenging or perplexing? In 1993, my husband, Ray, was stationed on the aircraft carrier, USS Carl Vinson ported at the Bremerton Naval Shipyard in Bremerton, Washington. It was decided to change the homeport of this ship to Alameda, California. In January of that year, thousands of Navy families were moved from the Puget Sound area of Washington State to the San Francisco Bay area. Because base housing was not immediately available, Ray had to put our then four-year-old daughter, Megan, and me in temporary housing in Vallejo, California. We quickly learned the *unofficial* name given to this housing complex by the residing military families as *Garbage Gardens*. Once we moved in, Ray returned to the ship to prepare for its relocation later that year.

For eight months we lived in 1940's transient housing for soldiers being deployed during World War II. At least that's the story we got. The housing units were made of concrete blocks running in a long parallel fashion, all connected one to another, much like box cars on a train, and painted battleship gray. Each unit had about 600 square feet of living space. On the lower floor were just two windows, one in the front and one in the back with vertical gray iron bars across them.

None of the units in our section had front yards, just a porch step to the parking lot. The backyard was something right out of a 1950's catalog— just one long stretch of grass and each unit's back door opened up to this common yard and clotheslines evenly spaced apart running the length of the units. Many of the military families living there owned dogs and the common yard area was not only the children's only play area, but also where the pets did their business. The nickname Garbage Gardens aptly described our lowly abode. It was not only a challenging place to live while we waited for our name to come to the top of the list for adequate housing, but it was equally dangerous. Garbage Gardens was in a rough area of the city. Those wishing to do harm knew that the inhabitants of these units were women with children whose husbands were stationed on ships and underway. It was not uncommon to see police in the housing areas making out incidence reports.

A week after Ray had returned to the U.S.S. Carl Vinson, I awoke one morning to find litter from a fast food chain strewn all over our front porch step. *How could this be happening? We just moved here,* I wondered, shaking my head in frustration. This insolent act was like getting a slap in the face. Dismayed, I headed for the kitchen to get the trash can. "This is definitely Garbage Gardens alright," I muttered in disgust, as I picked up empty wrappers, food cartons, and pieces of partially eaten food. Even though part of me was angry, thoughts of conceding to a miserable existence beat at the door of my heart. Everything about Garbage Gardens was a challenge. And my efforts to remain optimistic were equally challenged.

Like the psalmist in our first Psalm of Ascent, I had other *woe is me* moments during our stay at Garbage Gardens. I also felt like a foreigner in a strange land; I was a long way from where my heart wished to be.

Rescue Me, O Lord from False Accusers

The psalmist in our first Psalm of Ascent opens with a plea for help. He gives the reason for his distress: being a victim of someone's lies and deceit. It struck me odd that he choose to begin the collection of Psalms of Ascent with this topic. After all, Psalm 120 represents the beginning of the Israelites' journey to Jerusalem. When setting out on a trip, my thoughts usually turn first to the safety of the trip. When boarding a plane I pray for a well-rested flight crew, protection, and a mechanically sound airplane. When traveling by car I pray for a hedge of protection on the roads. However, for the Israelites, traveling in caravans with others for days or weeks, refraining from ungodly speech was an important issue.

Walter C. Kaiser, Jr. in his book, *The Journey Isn't Over,* quotes Samuel Cox in his 1885 exposition of theses psalms (*The Pilgrim Psalms: An Exposition of the Songs of Degrees*, London: R.D. Dickinson, 1885). Cox sheds light on the possibility of why the psalmist began with this particular distress call. He says,

> "It is hardly an exaggeration to say that half of the miseries of human life spring from the reckless and malignant use of the tongue. And these wicked tongues generally wag fastest behind a (person's) back, amid the excitement of social intercourse. We judge these sins of the tongue all too lightly, until we ourselves are injured by them."

As the Israelites left their homes for the journey to the Holy City, it is highly probable they prayed for strength to withstand the temptation of all forms of malicious talk while in the joyous company of other Israelites.

It comes as no surprise that Christians in the military are confronted with a fair amount of foul language and twisted humor. Christian military members are no different than their non-Christian cohorts in that they desire to have a sense of camaraderie within a group of peers. Yet, the temptation is strong to join in on a crude joke, slanderous talk about another service member, or succumb to gossip. And if not controlled, this unattractive habit becomes toxic, destroying character. Just as unflattering speech reveals a person's character, it also exposes how we truly feel about God. Likewise, the men and women of our armed forces who demonstrate restraint when assaulted verbally not only reflect positively on themselves, but also reflects positively on our country's image worldwide. No amount of slanderous talk or deceit is worth losing one's integrity.

The Word of God has volumes to say about the use of the tongue. Let's start with the basics—the Ten Commandments. "You shall not bear false witness against your neighbor" (Exodus 20:16). God established this command to protect the reputation of people from defamation.[4] Additionally, it became the building blocks for the Israelites' system of justice.[5] Bearing false witness means giving untrue testimony in court.[6] It also means that we are to be honest in all of our transactions with others. Bearing false witness can also include twisting the truth, deception through dishonesty, fraud, cheating, and lying. Jesus is the Spirit of Truth (John 16:13). And when we speak in truth, we are in agreement with Him. In John 8:44 Satan is called the father of lies. And when we lie or deceive someone, we are a participant of Satan's court.

When my kids were small I began reading, *The Power of A Praying Parent* by Stormie Omartian. I was particularly interested in the chapter on lying. I wanted to know how to handle lying with a godly approach. In her book I found what was needed to help my son, Lawrence, understand why God hates sin. Stormie says, "Every time you lie you give Satan a piece of your heart." Ouch! Those twelve words was all it took for Lawrence to grasp the magnitude of lying and the unattractive consequences. Even I had never thought of lying in that way.

Lying and deceit erodes trust in a family, but it is equally true for all levels of the military ranks. Giving a false testimony or lying behind another service member's back is damaging and breaks down the cohesion of the entire group, team or unit. And when deceptive speech and lying become a habit, the integrity of that person suffers. Sadly, a habit of lying also weakens and devalues our relationship with God. The Bible says, "The getting of treasures by a lying tongue is a fleeting vapor and a snare of death" (Proverbs 21:6). In other words, there may be something gained by lying, but it is short lived. Its temporary value will ultimately return to zero. [7]

> **KEY POINT #2**
>
> There may be something gained by lying, but it is short lived. Its temporary value returns to zero.

So, what does our psalmist say about lying lips and a deceitful tongue? There are a couple of ways to glean the meaning of verses 2 through 4 of Psalm 120 and both are plausible. First, lying lips and a deceitful tongue can be compared to sharp arrows. A deceitful tongue, like arrows, cuts deeply which also leaves behind a lingering sting. Now, consider the second part of verse 4: "with glowing coals of the broom tree!" The broom tree is a large desert shrub that adapts to dry conditions. It is said that when burned, the coals from the broom tree retain their heat.[8] In the same way, if you touch hot coals, there's instant pain, and the burn left behind also leaves an irritating sting, just as slanderous words do.[9]

The second way we can interpret this metaphor is to view the arrows as God's quick and sharp judgment for the author of lying lips and a deceitful tongue. In an online article by R. Tuck titled, "Coals of Juniper," provides us with this revealing insight:

> The woes that come on the slanderer shall be like "coals of juniper," which are "quick in flaming, fierce in blazing, and long in burning."[10]

But what about the victim of lying and deception? Lies and slander led our psalmist to feel as though he was in the wrong place, living in Meshech and Kedar with people who didn't worship his God. Being in the wrong company can make us feel alone. This is the perspective from which our psalmist expresses himself.

We see an example of deception played out in the ninth chapter of Joshua. After Moses died, Joshua became the new leader to take the Israelites into the Promised Land. Before arriving to Canaan, Joshua and his army were commissioned by God to travel from city to city destroying every trace of idol worship. Perhaps Joshua was still on an emotional high after his two victories in Ai and Jericho as his reason for failing to seek God's advice about the Hivites from the city of Gibeon. This one failed war campaign set in motion an unfortunate consequence for the Israelites. Earlier, in Deuteronomy 7:1-2, God instructed Israel to destroy the nations nearby to Canaan and spare those nations that were afar. God also allowed Israel to make treaties with cities that were far from them. When Joshua's victory over the cities of Ai and Jericho (Joshua

6–8) became known, the Hivites, fearing Joshua's army concocted a cleaver trick. In deceit, they presented themselves as weary travelers from a far-off country with worn out clothes, old wineskins that had been mended, broken down sandals, and moldy bread. The scheme was successful and they secured their treaty with Joshua, thereby securing their escape from being destroyed. God had included the Hivites as one of the groups of people slated for destruction (see Exodus 34:11; Deu.20:17) because they worshipped other gods. Commanding Joshua and his army to destroy them was God's just way of protecting the Israelites from being ruined by the idolatry and immorality of its enemies.

Even though Joshua was a brilliant military strategist and knew better to seek God's direction before leading his men into battle or in a binding agreement, he did a foolish thing and took matters into his own hands and established a treaty with the Hivites. He made a wrong decision based on appearances.

When the leaders realized their terrible mistake, the consequences were set. Regrettably, Joshua had to protect the Hivites from their enemies because they entered into an agreement with them and God required that vows be honored (see Leviticus 5:4). They had to tolerate the Hivites now that they were allied with them. Similarly, when we don't seek God's guidance on important matters, we can be deceived. Like Joshua, moving forward on a matter in which we haven't sought the Lord's counsel, or basing a decision entirely on appearances, can lead to awkward or unfortunate situations that can quickly turn into a major nuisance.

Depending on which side of the fence we find ourselves—guilty of speaking untruth, or like our psalmist, the victim of lies and deception, God hasn't changed or compromised His natural law of sowing and reaping for Christians today. In Galations 6:7–8, the apostle Paul tells us that if we sow to our own flesh (continually seeking to please our own sinful desires), our crops will be destruction and sadness. Jesus is our example of how the believer is to sow. The seed is God's Word, but the type of soil the seed is planted in determines the type of harvest produced.

So, what is the Christian military member or family to do when a victim of slanderous talk or deception? The psalmist in verse 7 steers us in the direction to seek peace. He says, "I am for peace; but when I speak, they are for war." We can take our complaint to God in prayer, then seek out what the Bible has to say on the subject. We can also look to Jesus' example. First Peter 2:23 is a good place to start: "When he was abused, he did not return abuse; when he suffered, he did not threaten; but he entrusted himself to the one who judges justly." The Bible encourages us to let God deal directly with the one who has deceived us or spoken untruth concerning us. If we struggle with the temptation of falsehood and deceit, we must take our distress to God and ask Him to deliver us from it. Whether you are the service member, spouse of one, or family member, forming relationships with other brothers and sisters in Christ creates a strong bond that supports our daily walk with the Lord.

As Christians, working or living in environments that are indifferent to a faith in God, such as the military, we have to be prepared to face a certain amount of unjust suffering, but again we have Jesus as our example. He didn't retaliate in the suffering He endured. Just as the uniform the military member wears represents the United States, in the same way Christians represent our Savior Jesus Christ. Our goal is always to be moving towards Christ-likeness. We may want to seek retaliation, but this isn't God's method for us. As

---

KEY POINT #3

Just as the uniform the military member wears represents the United States, in the same way Christians represent Christ.

believers, we can instead place our trust in the promise found in Exodus 14:14: "The LORD will fight for you, and you shall hold your peace."

Since the United States has the finest military force in the world–turning out skilled leaders and warriors, men and women trained for battle, combined with courage, strength, and precision, adding godly conduct creates an elite fighting force with worldwide respect.

Prayer for Right Speech

Lord,

You are a God of mercy and I am thankful that when I call out to You in my distress, You are there. I pray that You would give me a heart that loves truth. I know that all lies originate with Satan and I ask You to remove any lying spirit within me. I confess those times that I have lied or deceived. Strengthen me to avoid flirting with the temptation to lie, deceive, or partake of ungodly speech for I am Your child, a member of Your Kingdom of Truth.

Help me to stop and think before I speak so that I can consider my words. Help me not to adopt a deceitful tongue or use slanderous words. May they have no place in my vocabulary. Instead, I pray that my words would bring honor to You.

As a member of the armed forces (or spouse or family member of a military member), let my words be encouraging. Help me to speak life instead of death and lead by Your example. Bring awareness to our military to reflect a godly example by speaking up for truth. Let there also be protection in that. Help me to live honestly so that by my example, my children will do the same. I ask that Your Spirit of Truth would guide me as it says in John 16:13. Let me be an agent of peace, but without compromising my faith or integrity. Amen

Chapter One Key Points

1. There are times in life when we must take God at His Word and trust in His promises.
2. Something may be gained by lying, but it is short-lived. Its temporary value returns to zero.
3. Just as the uniform the military member wears represents the United States, in the same way Christians represent Christ.

Reader's Reflections

1. Do you think God still punishes New Testament Christians by aiming His arrows back at those guilty for lying or deception?
2. Do you agree or disagree that one of the chief issues in the military is the use of the tongue? If so, why do you think this is? In your experience, how does the military handle lying and deceptive speech within its ranks?

Psalm of Strength

"Vindicate me, O Lord, for I have walked in my integrity,
and I have trusted in the LORD without wavering."

Psalm 26:1

PSALM OF ASCENT 121

¹ I lift up my eyes to the hills–
    from where will my help come?
² My help comes from the Lord,
    who made heaven and earth.
³ He will not let your foot be moved;
    he who keeps you will not slumber.
⁴ He who keeps Israel
    will neither slumber nor sleep.
⁵ The Lord is your keeper;
    the Lord is your shade at your right hand.
⁶ The sun shall not strike you by day,
    nor the moon by night.
⁷ The Lord will keep you from all evil;
    he will keep your life.
⁸ The Lord will keep
        your going out and your coming in
        from this time on and forevermore.

DANGER LURKS

My help comes from the LORD, who made heaven and earth.

Psalm 121:2

What does the word *security* mean to you? This concept can mean different things to different people. During the years of the Great Recession, the United States experienced a great deal of fear and insecurity. Trust in established systems eroded away as we watched the world's economy plummet, tearing a gaping hole in our safety nets. What we once thought were *guarantees* became empty promises–And it is still unclear what it will take to plug the hole. Thankfully, God's promises to believers will never fall victim to this world's ways and its imperfect systems. His Word is His promise.

17

The theme for our second Psalm of Ascent is the security the pilgrims had from God's tireless care. The journey to the temple in Jerusalem was difficult and potentially dangerous. The pilgrims walked all day and were exposed to the elements. No rest stops dotted the barren landscape for them to load up on water or seek reprieve from the hot sun. To avoid the sun's heat, many walked by night. But this only brought on apprehension about the dangers facing them that they couldn't detect. Being alert to possible raids by their enemies was paramount as it wasn't uncommon for enemy forces to take Israelite prisoners after their raids.[1] "Now the Arameans on one of their raids had taken a young girl captive from the land of Israel, and she served Naaman's wife" (2 Kings 5:2). If that didn't provoke insecurity amongst the traveling Israelites, not knowing what lurked in the surrounding mountains no doubt did.

God is the Source of Our Help

In the first two verses, the psalmist acknowledges that he looks up to the surrounding mountains. His help is not from the mountains, but lifting his gaze up to the hills represented his help came from above—heaven. Israel depended on God as their Source of help. In looking up to the hills, they saw them as mighty and stable, reminding them of their God. The psalmist underscores how monumental his God is by calling attention to the work He did in creating heaven and earth: "My help comes from the LORD, who made heaven and earth" (121.1). If God created heaven and earth, He was certainly qualified to be the Source of the pilgrim's help. The prophet, Jeremiah, also spoke of his all-powerful God. "Ah, Lord GOD! It is you who made the heavens and the earth by your great power and by your outstretched arm! Nothing is too hard for you" (Jeremiah 32:17).

Second Chronicles 20 tells of the story of a king who found himself in a dire crises upon learning that his country was about to be invaded. King Jehoshaphat, one of Judah's better kings, demonstrated great faith before God and his people while in an ominous predicament. "He walked in the way of his father Asa and did not turn aside from it, doing what was right in the sight of the LORD" (2 Chronicles 20:32).

The people of Judah had a history of an inconsistent faith, wavering between obedience and rebellion. The spiritual climate was ultimately determined by whatever king was reigning at the time.[2] Thus, the nation had a mixture of good and bad kings with varying degrees in between. The fundamental premise that qualified a king as good was represented by eliminating idol worship and faithfully keeping to God's decrees. Jehoshaphat was among the good kings for another reason. He understood the correlation between obedience to God's standards and success in his kingdom.

Our story begins when Jehoshaphat is warned about the armies of the Moabites and the Ammonites, coming against him for battle. Deeply distraught, he alerts his people to seek God's help through a time of fasting. Jehoshaphat knew that if he had God's favor, God would hear his cries for help and bring victory against the approaching armies. In not knowing what to do, Jehoshaphat sought God first. In doing so, he did three wise things:

1. **He acknowledged God's power and might**. "O LORD, God of our ancestors, are you not God in heaven? Do you not rule over all the kingdoms of the nations? In your hand are power and might, so that no one is able to withstand you"(2 Chronicles 20:6).

2. **He reminds his people of God's past care and help**. "Did you not, O our God, drive out the inhabitants of this land before your people Israel, and give it forever to the descendants of your friend Abraham?" (2 Chronicles 20:7).

3. **He acknowledged his dependence on God**. "O our God, will you not execute judgment upon them? For we are powerless against this great multitude that is coming against us. We do not know what to do, but our eyes are on you" (2 Chronicles 20:12).

King Jehoshaphat displayed great humility before his people who came from all across Judah to support him. He pleaded with his people to pray like never before, and God responded to their petitions for help. From the multitudes gathered, God raised up a man by the name of Jahaziel to deliver His message to the Israelites. It was a combination of a pep talk to turn the people's dread into hope, and an answer to King Jehoshaphat's humble prayer. Jahaziel said, "Listen, all Judah and inhabitants of Jerusalem, and King Jehoshaphat: Thus says the LORD to you: 'Do not fear or be dismayed at this great multitude; for the battle is not yours but God's' " (2 Chronicles 20:15). Jahaziel instructed the people to be willing participants by confronting their enemy–not as soldiers, but instead as an army of prayer warriors.[3] God, the all powerful Warrior assured them that this battle was His. He destroyed the Moabites and the Ammonites by creating confusion and panic to run rampant within enemy forces causing them to kill one another. Just as He promised God secured Judah's victory.

America is unique in that it has never been occupied by enemy forces. In the Old Testament, the threat of one kingdom invading another was a constant danger. Jehoshaphat knew his army was insufficient to conquer his enemies. In humility, he admitted before God and his people that he didn't know what to do (2 Chronicles 20:12). Ponder on that for a moment. This king did not have a plan! It is no wonder his people were in despair over the armies bearing down on them. Can you imagine if the President of the United

States declared to the people of this country that our military lacked sufficient fighting power to defend itself against her enemies? Would the people of this nation fall to their knees in humble prayer for God to respond? Has America been a nation that has given God a place of honor within our government and within our homes, and made Him Lord over our lives to know with all confidence that God would intervene on our behalf? These are questions many Christians ask in light of America's spiritual decline. Because the United States was founded by people who depended on God and submitted to His authority, America has been a blessed nation.

KEY POINT #1

There still exists a relationship between a country that honors and depends on God, and having His blessing.

Psalm 33:12 says: "Blessed is the nation whose God is the LORD, the people He has chosen as His own inheritance" (NKJV). God's Word has not changed through the centuries; there still exists a relationship between a country that honors and depends on God, and having His blessing. Pastor David Jeremiah, in his book, *What in the World is Going On?* quotes Benjamin Franklin who said: "The longer I live, the more convincing proofs I see of the truth–that God governs in the affairs of Men. And," he continued, "without His aid, we shall succeed in this political building no better than the builders of Babel."[4]

It is a daunting thought that as America keeps taking steps to move out from under God's authority, we cannot expect Him to keep blessing this nation. In Second Chronicles 7:14 God beckons His people to heed his invitation: "If my people who are called by my name humble themselves, pray, seek my face, and turn from their wicked ways, then I will hear from heaven, and will forgive their sin and heal their land."

God knows we can be needy people. He designed us that way so we would recognize Him as our Source of help, no matter how simple or dire our situation. He didn't create us just to abandon us to figure life out on our own. All matters of His children are of great concern to Him.

The LORD is Your Keeper

The word *keep* is used six times in Psalm 121. The psalmist did not want us to miss the importance of this promise. The word for *keep* in Hebrew is *shamar* (shaw-mar), meaning to *watch over with great care*, to *protect*, *attend to*, to *preserve*.[5] The psalmist identifies God as the great Keeper of our lives. This pledge extended the length of the pilgrim's lives (v.8). It was imperative they kept God's promise of protection always before them as a reminder that their lives were in the hands of their Keeper.

This promise is ours too. God remains the Keeper of those whose hearts are His. When our armed forces seek God and place their trust in Him, they partake in God's promises. Second Corinthians 1:20 says, "For in him [Jesus] every one of God's promises is a "Yes." Jesus carried out His heavenly Father's ministry faithfully. He fulfilled all of His promises, even the promise to give up His life for us. If Jesus was faithful in trading His life for ours, why would believers ever doubt that God wouldn't be with our loved ones serving in harm's way? As our Keeper, God isn't limited to protecting our physical bodies, but He is also the Keeper of our faith, protecting it from deception by Satan. God's protection is all-inclusive.

Unlike today, the pilgrims probably had just one type of shoe to walk in. Perhaps verse 3 came to the psalmist because he

---

TODAY'S PEARL

"He will not let your foot be moved; he who keeps you will not slumber" (Psalm 121:3).

was on this journey by foot. "He will not let your foot be moved; he who keeps you will not slumber." The terrain could be treacherous and the Israelites had to be mindful of where they placed their feet. This verse reflects overtones of security in three ways: protecting them physically from slipping on the difficult terrain, shielding them from outside dangers that had the potential of shaking them off their feet, and showing them that God isn't limited by space (omnipresent). He is not a lesser god who sleeps.

While my husband was on active duty we enjoyed the privilege of Dependent's Day Cruises as a Navy family. These cruises allowed families and friends of crew members to come aboard ship to get a feel for life on a war vessel. In the early morning hours, hundreds of family members and friends descend upon the ship. Once on board, the lines are dropped and the ship leaves the pier. While underway the ship provides meals, music, and a spectacular up-close air show of Navy jets doing "touch and goes" on the flight deck. It's a day in which sailors and their families forget about the rigorous ship schedules, training missions and deployments, and enjoy this one-of-a-kind experience. Pride in our sailor, pride in our Navy, and pride in our country is refreshed in our hearts and we reflect that we are a part of something unique and important.

On this particular Dependent's Day Cruise, my husband, Ray, was stationed on the aircraft carrier the USS Abraham Lincoln. He led us down steep ladders from one deck to another as he gave us the guided tour. My mother-in-law, Marilyn–who was visiting at the time–became claustrophobic as the spaces seemed to get smaller and smaller the further we descended. Finally, she turned around and returned to the security of the surface. The rest of us found ourselves in a small square room called the pump room, far below the waterline. There, all alone, was a sailor on his watch. However, he had fallen victim to the dead silence and was sound asleep. Our loud voices upon entering had suddenly awakened him, a fact he was probably thankful for later.

Falling asleep on a watch is a serious matter in the military, often resulting in stiff penalties. Thankfully, with God that will never happen. He alone stands the "***duty watch***" 24/7. He is never found asleep. He is never caught off guard and nothing escapes His attention.

As a Christian military family, it's important to give your anxieties over the safety of your loved one in a foreign or hostile environment to the Lord. If anxieties are allowed to fester, doubt crowds out trust and your relationship with God suffers. To keep insecurity and fears of the unknown from gaining a foothold on your heart, training is key. Like military training, spiritual training should be included in the military family's readiness regimen. Faith truly makes a difference when confronted with the threat of danger. This type of training involves two things: living close, or abiding, in the Lord, and having a consistent prayer routine. With God as the fortress of our hearts, our faith is girded up and made more resilient.

> **KEY POINT #2**
>
> Consistently renewing your mind with God's Word empowers you to resist the temptation to allow fears of what *could* happen to cause you to doubt God's protective care.

How do we make God the fortress of our heart? We begin by reading God's Word. James 4:8 says: "Draw near to God and He will draw near to you." His Word is sustenance for our souls. Consistently renewing your mind with God's Word empowers you to resist the temptation to allow fears of what *could* happen to cause you to doubt God's protective care. By bathing in God's Word we gain a daily benefit. He gives us His peace. "You will keep him in perfect peace, Whose mind is stayed on You, Because he trusts in You" (Isaiah 26:3 NKJV). Neglecting God's Word allows your mind to become vulnerable to attacks from Satan. And what does Satan do best? He steals (see John 10:10). He will steal your peace if your mind and heart is not guarded by the power of God's Word. His peace stomps out fear.

Prayer is the second requirement for spiritual readiness training. Think of prayer as a shield, a fundamental ingredient to having God's protection. When we are covering our service member by the shield of prayer, we are engaging God's defense system of protection. When we place our military members into God's care through prayer, His power penetrates that which we are praying over. Prayer is the channel that allows God's grace and protection to invade the lives of our men and women in uniform.

KEY POINT #3

When we are covering our service member by the shield of prayer, we are engaging God's defense system of protection.

Part of having the umbrella of God's protection also includes living a life that is compliant to God's Word. Recall that King Jehoshaphat had God's favor because he followed God's ways which secured his victory over his enemies. Because obedience to God's Word is His will for believers, it should be our top priority–not because we have to, but because we want to out of love for the One who died for us. "Whoever keeps His word, truly the love of God is perfected in him. By this we know that we are in Him. He who says he abides in Him ought himself also to walk just as He walked" (1 John 2:5-6 NKJV). The more we become perfected in our obedience, the more we put it into practice through the circumstances of our lives.

Psalm 121 closes with this reminder: God's protection is without end–whether you wake up on unfriendly soil or on a ship in international waters, while on foot patrol in the light of day or in the darkness of the night, upon returning from a mission or home to the arms of waiting family. Throughout all circumstances, God's watchful care is limitless. If harm or an accident does touch our lives, we can draw upon the peace our Lord offers because we have prayed for His presence to be in the midst of it. Our assurance comes from knowing that nothing happens to those whose hearts belong to God that first hasn't passed through the sovereign hands of our Keeper. Embrace God and trust Him as the Keeper of your life and that of your beloved military member.

Prayer for Protection

Lord,

If I can't understand Your ways, I can take comfort in the truth of Psalm 25:10. "All the paths of the Lord are steadfast love and faithfulness, for those who keep his covenant and his decrees."

Thank You, Lord, for every member of our armed forces. Each one serves from the heart with a strong sense of duty for his or her country. Each one has voluntarily given up certain freedoms in order to answer to a higher calling. Lord, may their sacrifices be appreciated by the citizens of this country. Bring a revival in the hearts of the people of America to pray for our military so that under God we remain the strongest military force. May each military operation be just and carried out with a clear and honorable vision.

The challenges are many, Lord, and I pray for daily strength as they march into unknown dangers. Arm them with courage, shield each one from evil intentions, injustice, deceptive tactics, and reveal every unknown threat that would undermine their safety and the mission. Protect their feet from slipping (Psalm 121:3), no matter where they are, no matter the circumstances. In the light of day or the darkness of night, shield them with Your protection. When exhausted, be their Source of strength.

Lord, like You did for the pilgrims traveling to Jerusalem be the Keeper of our men and women in uniform (Psalm 121:5). Should any return home wounded, physically or from the effects of posttraumatic stress syndrome, I pray that immediate help would be theirs for a complete healing and for the return of a sound mind. For those who have already given the ultimate sacrifice, comfort their families by encamping around their hurting hearts.

Faithful Father, the steadfast love of the Lord never ceases, His mercies never come to an end; they are new every morning" (see Lamentations 3:22). May the mercy You provide be experienced by my loved one and all our troops. Let Your compassion be theirs and give them opportunities to see Your faithfulness daily. Psalm 25:21 says: "May integrity and uprightness preserve me." May our military leadership be men and women who value Your vital role in the affairs of our country. May our military commanders call on You for guidance, and give them understanding of things they don't know (Jeremiah 33:3). In doing so, may Your name be exalted. In addition to physical readiness, may our leaders be dedicated to preparing our service members with spiritual readiness, so faith can make a difference. Amen.

Chapter Two Key Points

1. There still exists a relationship between a country that honors and depends on God and having His blessing.
2. Consistently renewing your mind with God's Word empowers you to resist the temptation to allow fears of what *could* happen to cause you to doubt God's protective care.
3. Think of prayer as a shield for protection. When we are covering our service member by the shield of prayer, we are engaging God's defense system of protection.

Reader's Reflections

1. What evidence do you see in our world today of countries who have removed God as the over-ruling authority? Does this evidence point to God removing His hand of blessing?

2. Besides physical protection, what other ways is God our Keeper?

3. As the military member, how has God demonstrated His position as the Keeper of your life? If you are the spouse or family member of a loved one serving in the armed forces, in what ways has God been your Source of help and the Keeper of your life while separated by deployments?

4. As a Christian military family, how do you handle your anxieties over the safety of your loved one in a foreign or unfriendly environment? Is prayer and reading God's Word a regular part of your daily schedule?

Psalm of Strength

"He shall cover you with His feathers, And under His wings you shall take refuge; His truth shall be your shield and buckler"

(Psalm 91:4 NKJV).

PSALM OF ASCENT 122

[1] I was glad when they said to me,
    "Let us go to the house of the Lord!"
[2] Our feet are standing
    within your gates, O Jerusalem.
[3] Jerusalem—built as a city
    that is bound firmly together.
[4] To it the tribes of the Lord,
    the tribes of the Lord,
    as was decreed for Israel,
    to give thanks to the name of the Lord.
[5] For there the thrones for judgment were set up,
    the thrones of the house of David.
[6] Pray for the peace of Jerusalem:
    "May they prosper who love you.
[7] Peace be within your walls,
    and security within your towers."
[8] For the sake of my relatives and friends
    I will say, "Peace be within you."
[9] For the sake of the house of the Lord our God,
    I will seek your good.

LET US GO TO THE HOUSE OF THE Lord

I was glad when they said to me,
"Let us go to the House of the Lord!"
Psalm 122:1

Have you ever traveled to a place that you couldn't believe you were actually there? For me it was traveling to Egypt as a teenager. From my home in Kansas I couldn't contemplate scaling up and down the massive boulders of the Great Pyramids of Giza, or standing in front of the largest statue in the world made out of limestone, the Great Sphinx, and seeing with my own eyes the inside of the tomb of King Tutankhamun. For a girl who loved ancient history, this trip was the epitome of all history lessons.

Our psalmist, King David, who penned the third Psalm of Ascent expresses his own enthusiasm for reaching Jerusalem much the same way as I did about my trip to Egypt. His body was tired, his feet ached, but he barely noticed because his heart was joyful at the realization that he had arrived in his beloved city. "Our feet are standing within your gates, O Jerusalem" (Psalm 122:1–2). At last the psalmist was there, in the company of other pilgrims doing what his heart loved most: worshipping inside the great temple that had been designated as God's spiritual dwelling place.

In complete delight and awe, David marvels at the layout of the city, notably how compressed it is. "Jerusalem–built as a city that is bound firmly together" (v.3). He likens the city's compact structure to the multitude of pilgrims pressed together in authentic unity and fellowship. Like these early pilgrims, our homes, too, ought to be firmly bound together in one accord for the Lord.

King David's devotion to the Lord was more than genuine; he was passionate about being in the presence of his God. There is little doubt that he was delighted to be invited by others to worship God together. David knew that true worship–having a heart to heart encounter with God pleased Him. How about you? When invited to go to church, how do you react? Do you respond like David, thrilled by the invitation? Or do you wince at the thought of losing the easy, lazy Sunday morning feel? I can identify with David's enthusiasm for attending worship services. Active in my church youth group, I have always loved church. It was in that body of believers that I caught the fervor of the Lord. I craved the spiritual energy that projected from my church experience. As a college freshman, I joined Campus Christians and lived in an old federal style three-story fraternity house. It was converted into co-ed living quarters for Christian students that attended the University of Kansas. Today, after a busy week in our family business, I look forward to church for the spiritual refreshment, learning how to apply Bible truth to real life, worship and fellowship.

Drifting Off Course

So why all the fuss about church attendance? Plain and simple, it's God's desire that believers meet consistently with other believers. God didn't wire us to live the Christian life in a self-sufficient or solitary manner. There are two good reasons for this:

First, to protect our hearts from drifting.[1] This world is bursting with influences that can easily take us off course. By making church attendance a vital part of our faith, we remain in the channel that safeguards us against drifting. Every believer needs a church home. Ephesians 2:19 says: "But you are citizens with the saints and also members of the household of God." Within the church body, we make spiritual connections with other believers. When we serve and do for others, we are serving Jesus (see Matthew 25:37-40). This teaches us to be committed and dependent on one another in the church body. Then when we hit rough seas we are less likely to veer off.

KEY POINT #1

By making church attendance a vital part of our faith, we remain in the channel that safeguards us against drifting off course.

Because of the spiritual connections you make within the body of believers at your local church, you have established valuable lifelines for reaching out for help and support. Just as you and your family are part of the larger military family with a network of support systems to assist your military lifestyle, so too, does the church; it offers the spiritual grit you'll need when military life gets downright hard, lonely, or overwhelming. If you don't have a church home yet, seek one out that offers a military ministry. Due in large part to the Iraq and Afghanistan wars, many churches today are recognizing the need for military ministries to meet the unique spiritual and material needs of military families.

Although securing spiritual connections with fellow believers and with God is imperative, it is not enough. For spiritual growth to occur it takes more than taking up a seat in the church pew Sunday after Sunday. Spiritual muscle is produced by becoming an active participant in a local church.[2] Our participation within the church also allows God to show us opportunities that He may have for us. Each member brings a certain aspect of Christ's character and a skill set to the body in service to others. Every believer has something to offer the church body, and the more it is utilized in service to others the greater the appreciation of the body of Christ.

God takes drifting away from Him seriously. James 5:19-20 says: "My brothers and sisters, if anyone among you wanders from the truth and is brought back by another, you should know that whoever brings back a sinner from wandering will save the sinner's soul from death and will cover a multitude of sins." Jesus gave us the charge to bring those who have drifted away back to Him. Rick Warren, in his book, *The Purpose Driven Life* states, "The Christian life is more than just commitment to Christ; it includes a commitment to other Christians."[3] When a believer drifts away from his faith, he is at a greater risk to Satan's tactics because his spiritual muscles have weakened. Drifting, if not corrected will lead to complacency in spiritual matters.

Complacency–A Slow Spiritual Death

The second reason for church attendance is to prevent a sense of complacency, or indifference to settle in our hearts. The Merriam-Webster's Collegiate Dictionary gives the definition of complacency as, "self-satisfaction especially when accompanied by unawareness of actual dangers or deficiencies."[4] Complacency causes our spiritual life to shift its focus from God to ourselves. "Your participation in a local church protects your personal fellowship with God.[5] When you drift away from the family of God, it is only a matter of time until you drift away from fellowship with God."[6]

The antidote for complacency is Romans 12:11. "Do not lag in zeal, be ardent in spirit, serve the Lord." Another word for a complacent believer is the lukewarm Christian. And a lukewarm Christian becomes an uncommitted Christian. He sits on the fence without a strong conviction on the causes of Christ. If this condition persists, one becomes self-satisfied and the process of decay begins.

KEY POINT #2

Complacency is a state of idleness that prevents growth. It means we get comfortable with things the way they are and we compromise our faith.

What would of happened if the disciples returned to their former lives and allowed complacency to settle in their hearts after Christ's resurrection? Would we have the New Testament? Complacency is an unwillingness to act, or try new things when a situation calls for it. Complacency is a state of idleness that prevents growth. It means we get comfortable with things the way they are and we compromise our faith.

It is the same for a church. Do we settle for the same order or the same things, the same people doing the same functions, the same ministries, and programs. There's nothing wrong if those things are moving the church forward and growth occurs, but if not, why not? In a nutshell, complacency stifles growth, whether it is in our own lives or the life of the church. When complacency becomes the norm, or the status quo, we've allowed our spiritual condition to corrode. Christ rejected the status quo. He challenged his disciples to think outside the box, to do and see things with a different perspective–an eternal perspective so hearts would change. As believers, we have to be alert to the trappings of a complacent lifestyle. The majority of Americans live in a materialistic, comfortable, and a war-free existence that it requires a concerted effort to not subscribe to a complacent mindset. This world offers temporary satisfactions such as money, material possessions, and a pleasurable lifestyle that has the potential to leave us feeling indifferent to church, to God, or to the Bible.[7] If you find yourself feeling indifferent to those things, you have begun to shut God out of your life.[8] Complacency is a subtle heart killer. When a society becomes complacent, it lets its guard down and becomes vulnerable to unforeseen threats.

America didn't become the greatest fighting force in the world from using old ways of training for battle. As war changed, the military adapted.

> **KEY POINT #3**
>
> Our military cannot remain idle or subscribe to a complacent attitude towards its threats. It is the same with our faith. We often fight an unseen foe and we must stay vigilant if we desire victory.

As new threats appear on the horizon, our country's defense system has the responsibility to discover new ways to deal with them. To do nothing is to succumb to defeat. Our armed forces cannot remain idle or subscribe to a complacent attitude towards its threats. It is the same with our faith. We often fight an unseen foe and we must stay vigilant if we desire victory in our spiritual life. Just as the military pursues excellence, Christians must also pursue excellence in their faith with a passionate heart for God. Revelation 3:19 says: "therefore be zealous and repent." God's instructions are not like a buffet line, in which we can choose which attributes of Christian character we'll put on, but rather they are commands. God knows our struggle with complacency. And He has given us the cure. We are wise to assess the spiritual condition of our hearts.

If you're in spiritual decline, Jesus is patiently waiting for you to ask Him back in. He pursues you, by knocking on the door of your heart, but He won't force open the door. "My wayward children," says the LORD, "come back to me, and I will heal your wayward hearts" (Jeremiah 3:22 NLT). Jesus longs to be back in your heart by a humble invitation. If you've been away from Him and would like to invite Jesus in, pray:

Lord, I want to come back to You. I am sorry for allowing my heart to drift. I am sorry I have endorsed a complacent mindset. Forgive me. With a humble spirit, I invite you back in. Please reignite my faith with an ardent spirit so that my life and faith will make a difference. Remove all indifference within me and replace it with a faith that is zealous in spirit. Give me a heart like David's that thirsts for You and Your Word. Amen.

If you prayed that prayer, it is important that you seek out a local church that is alive with the Holy Spirit and makes you feel welcomed. Worshipping our Lord with other believers breathes life into our faith. It is where you'll be supported and guided by biblical perspectives, and be affirmed in your faith. This is the one place where Christians, no matter where they're stationed can meet together in Christ's love and acceptance. Worship and fellowship in the company of other believers prevents the light that is within us from diminishing.

In verse 4 David reminds us of who authored the annual festivals. In Leviticus 23:1 God charged Moses with the job of telling the Israelites about the holy festivals and how they were to be honored each year. It is these festivals David is referring to in verse 4. "To it the tribes go up, the tribes of the LORD, as was decreed for Israel, to give thanks to the name of the LORD." God's intentions for these festivals was to be for times of celebrating with Him as a reminder of all He had done for them.[9] Annually, the tribes of Israel came together as one nation under God to fellowship, find rest, and refreshment.[10] Here we see God creating community and fellowship.

In an environment where the purpose was for giving thanks to God, there wasn't room for pride. Pride causes fellowship to collapse. For the Israelites, the only attitude for such an occasion was a humble one. In our society, I have noticed a gap between the older generation and the younger generation. That gap is called humility. Pride can get in the way of the older generation relating to our young people and young people from valuing the wisdom of elders. First Peter 5:5 says: "Clothe yourselves with humility in your dealings with one another." Fellowship and community begins when we wear humility as our best suit.

The temple of Jerusalem not only represented the main attraction of the pilgrim's place of worship, but also where some decisions of the court were made. In instances where justice was unable to be determined, the case was referred to a temple priest.[11] The priest, being impartial had the final say.[12] David recalled these "thrones of judgment" in verse 5 of Psalm 122 to make the connection that worship and civil matters often blended under God's structure of justice. Thus, we can draw the conclusion that God's law had a place in their judicial system.

Jerusalem–Peace for the City

Out of devotion for the Holy City, David concludes with a plea to ask for prayer for peace in Jerusalem. "Pray for the peace of Jerusalem: 'May they prosper who love you. Peace be within your walls, and security within your towers'" (v.6–7). For those that prayed for Jerusalem, David said they would have God's blessing. The reason is given in verse 8. "For the sake of my relatives and friends, I will say, 'Peace be within you.' "For the sake of the house of the LORD our God, I will seek your good." David was looking down the road to future generations so that those who came after him, would have the joy of making the journey to worship in the temple for the annual festivals.

Peace for Israel is still elusive. It remains a country where religious friction still persists. His plea to pray for Jerusalem or the whole nation of Israel is just as timely today as it was in the psalmist's day. Christians today are encouraged to continue in David's example and pray for Israel. And while we're at it, we would do well to also pray for peace within the walls of our own homes, cities, and country.

Prayer of Peace for Israel

Lord,

I pray that Your truth and Your light would shine over the nation of Israel. From generation to generation, Israel still remains mired in conflict, where there is still much bloodshed. But You, O Lord remain in a covenant relationship with Israel because You are a Sovereign God and You do not break Your promises. I pray that You would protect Israel from all threats. May plans of harm not prevail against her. Let all plans of evil be revealed. You, O Lord rule over all nations. I bring before You the government of Israel. May they seek Your wisdom in all agreements with other governments. Provide clear and divine counsel. Strengthen those who stand guard over Israel. And protect all who defend her. Lord, may the people of Israel seek Your face for their shield of protection. Your Word says in Psalm 33:12, "Happy is the nation whose God is the LORD, the people whom he has chosen as his heritage." Amen.

Chapter Three Key Points

1. By making church attendance a vital part of our faith, we remain in the channel that safeguards us against drifting off course.

2. Complacency is a state of idleness that prevents growth. It means we get comfortable with things the way they are and we compromise our faith.

3. Our military cannot remain idle or subscribe to a complacent attitude towards its threats. It is the same with our faith. We often fight an unseen foe and we must stay vigilant if we desire victory.

Reader's Reflections

1. How would you characterize your faith right now? Is your faith like David's, passionate for the Lord? Or has it completely cooled?
2. How would you describe your view of going to church? Does it feel like a chore or do you enjoy going? If so, what is it that draws you back each time?
3. Have you ever considered the link between praying for the good and the peace of Jerusalem and God's blessings for those that do?

Psalm of Strength

"But for me it is good to be near God; I have made the Lord God my refuge, to tell of all your works"
(Psalm 73:28).

PSALM OF ASCENT 123

¹ To you I lift up my eyes,
    O you who are enthroned in the heavens!
² As the eyes of servants
        look to the hand of their master,
        as the eyes of a maid
        to the hand of her mistress,
        so our eyes look to the LORD our God,
        until he has mercy upon us.
³ Have mercy upon us, O LORD,
        have mercy upon us,
        for we have had more than enough of
        contempt.
⁴ Our soul has had more than its fill
        of the scorn of those who are at ease,
        of the contempt of the proud.

I LIFT MY EYES

As the eyes of servants look to the hand of their master,
as the eyes of a maid to the hand of her mistress, so our
eyes look to the LORD, our God, until he has mercy upon us.

Psalm 123:2

I t's unclear who the writer of Psalm 123 is, but popular opinion suggests King Hezekiah at the time of the invasion of Judah by the Assyrians. This psalm of Ascent is about sorrow—in particular, sorrow as a result of prolonged contempt. It's a psalm spoken on behalf of a community expressing their grief. And it provides us with a model for approaching God when we find ourselves as the objects of disrespect. Psalm 123 opens with a similar tone to Psalm 121–"I lift up my eyes to the hills." The focal point this time is on God's position-

TODAY'S PEARL

"Yet you are holy, enthroned
on the praises of Israel. In you
our ancestors trusted; they
trusted, and you delivered
them" (Psalm 22:3-4).

enthroned in heaven. It's a good reminder of His supremacy, the eternal Ruler overall.

The theme of this Psalm of Ascent is having an attentive heart to where God would lead us and His intervening power when we become the objects of someone's contempt. This short psalm is twofold: a complaint by a single pilgrim on behalf of the people of his nation, and (2) through the use of a metaphor in verse 2, the pilgrims convey their need for guidance and acknowledging their dependency on God's mercy.

History records how Israel has been the object of scorn and contempt for many centuries. Over time constant condemnation left the pilgrims feeling battered. Weary of constant disrespect and ridicule, they cried out for God's mercy. The word contempt means "willful disobedience to or open disrespect of a court, judge, or legislative body, a lack of respect or reverence for something, or the act of despising."[1] Have you ever been the object of someone's contempt? If so, then it is likely you can relate to the theme of this psalm.

King David knew a thing or two about contempt. Second Samuel 6:16 gives the account of King David's first wife, Michal. She was King Saul's daughter and an example of an ungodly wife. Chapter 6 tells the story of David's efforts to bring the Ark of the Covenant containing the Ten Commandments back to Jerusalem. However, it was in the home of Abinadad in Kiriath-jearim. When the Philistines defeated Israel (1 Samuel 4), they confiscated the ark. The Philistines worshipped many gods and if the ark was that important to the Israelites then it was worth taking. The Philistines also believed that the more gods on their side, the more secure they felt.[2] They were sadly mistaken. God will never share His glory with any other god. Therefore, He unleashed a deadly plague upon those Philistines who lived in close proximity to the ark. They became ill and died. The Philistines then relocated the ark to two more cities under Philistine rule, but in each location God brought on the same panic and calamity. Suddenly, no Philistine wanted anything to do with the ark, and they returned it to Israel where it ended up in the home of Abinadab.

Twenty years passed and after David became king of Israel, he set about to bring the Ark of the Covenant from the home of Abinadab back to Jerusalem (2 Samuel 6). He knew this would please God and would ensure the entire nation of God's blessing. Unfortunately, not everyone was as thrilled as David was at having the ark returned. Michal didn't share in her husband's joy nor did she have David's devotion to God.[3] She resented David's God. When the ark reached the city of David, "Michal daughter of Saul looked out of the window, and saw King David leaping and dancing before the LORD; and she despised him in her heart" (2 Samuel 6:16). Maybe Michal considered dancing and worshipping God in public to be inappropriate or befitting of a king. It didn't matter; she was embarrassed and annoyed by David's undignified public performance. She says in 2 Samuel 6:20: "How the king of Israel honored himself today, uncovering himself today before the eyes of his servants' maids, as any vulgar fellow might shamelessly uncover himself!" David's reply revealed not only his genuine love of God, but also an unsympathetic promise to his wife.

> It was before the LORD, who chose me in place of your father and all his household, to appoint me as prince over Israel, the people of the LORD, that I have danced before the LORD. I will make myself yet more contemptible than this, and I will be abased in my own eyes; but by the maids of

whom you have spoken, by them I shall be held in honor (2 Samuel 6:21-22).

David knew that God cared more for the inward state of his heart rather than outward appearances.[4] He displayed his joy for the Lord in the freedom of that truth. Michal, on the other hand, focused her attentions on outward appearances, and perhaps she was more concerned with how her husband's undignified behavior would reflect on her. To David's credit, he didn't have a care in the least about what he looked like to the public. And it should be the same way for us. Repeated contemptuous remarks made by others should not deter us from courteously expressing our faith towards God, even when others are present.[5] Sadly, for Michal it didn't turn out well. She never came around to accepting the place God had put her. Instead, she remained bitter. Her contempt for David and to God had a sad consequence. She remained childless, a condition that brought on its own share of cultural shame.

KEY POINT #1

Repeated contemptuous remarks made by others should not deter us from expressing our feelings towards God, even when others are present.

More Than Enough Contempt

Verbal assaults, slurs, and constant ridicule come at us for various reasons. As Christians, we already stand out from the crowd. We may get strange looks from other patrons at restaurants when we bow our heads and pray before eating. Unbelieving coworkers may dish out an insincere comment about how we trust in God to work out difficult situations instead of taking matters into our own hands. Lest we forget, the world is never short of people who mock Christians for their faith in Jesus. So, what does our psalmist say about it?

We get our hint from verse 2: "As the eyes of servants look to the hand of their master, as the eyes of a maid to the hand of her mistress so our eyes look to the LORD our God." The psalmist compares himself to a servant. Think about the role of servants. They maintain their focus on their master.[6] The maid watches her mistress' hands, anticipating her forthcoming guidance. Because the maid depends on her mistress for her needs, all mercy, or compassion, rests in the mistress' control. The maid must maintain her gaze on her mistress or risk missing her mercy and guidance. Now think about Jesus. He maintained His focus on His heavenly Father so He could receive direction for fulfilling the purposes of God. In order to do that, Jesus kept His eyes fixed on His heavenly Father.

Likewise, we are encouraged to do the same. In those times when we've had more than enough contempt—whether through unkind words or conveyed with an ugly tone—our response is to settle our eyes upon Jesus and seek His mercy and His guidance. God hears the cries of a heart wounded many times over. "The LORD is gracious and full of compassion" (Psalm 111:4 NKJV).

> **KEY POINT #2**
>
> In those times when we've had more than enough contempt—whether through unkind words or conveyed with an ugly tone—our personal response is to settle our eyes upon Jesus and seek His mercy and His guidance.

Is someone in your command mistreating you with disrespectful remarks that have you discouraged? In verse 3, the pilgrims on their journey to Jerusalem recall in song their ancestral oppression. "Have mercy upon us, O LORD, have mercy upon us, for we have had more than enough of contempt." We can do the same. In fact, to make this petition for God to intervene more personal, replace the pronouns "us" with the pronouns "me" and "I." For example, "Have mercy upon [me], O LORD, have mercy upon [me], for [I] have had more than enough of contempt."

Often in my prayer journal, I write out my prayers for God's guidance in this way. Psalm 123 is our green light to come before Him, unpretentiously, for His favor. Does your military marriage resemble a battlefield, sabotaging you with frequent verbal landmines? Seeking support and services from resources within the military may be required, but God desires to be included in the circumstances of your life. Ask Him to bring about an end to the disdain. Ask God to guide and intervene. In situations where you have had more than enough contempt, go to your heavenly Father and ask for His mercy, His guidance, and deliverance. See the contempt from God's angle—from the standpoint of His power to defend and shield you. Like the "eyes of a maid to the hand of her mistress" (v. 3) we are to fix our eyes on our Master, watching intently for any hint of what His hands will do in our contemptuous situations. Many times over, God showed His mercy to the Israelites while under the harsh rule of their oppressors. When they cried out to God, He was moved by compassion and intervened. Yet, God didn't stop there. He sent Jesus so we would have an example. Jesus showed particular compassion for those who were objects of contempt. He mingled with them. He ate with them. He showed all mankind how to treat others. Yet, Jesus was the object of contempt as well. For this reason, He understands a heart wounded by contempt. Invite Him in the midst of your struggle and, like our psalmist, ask Him to intervene and to show you His mercy. If this speaks to your heart, He's waiting to hear from you.

If the contempt is severe enough, and you feel you cannot continue to endure under it, I encourage you to seek a biblical perspective from a trained Christian counselor. It may be a necessary first step.

You may be familiar with a concept known as "Familiarity Breeds Contempt." Its basic premise states that the more an employee gets to know his supervisor or someone who holds a superior position, the more likely that person is to find fault with him.[7] This concept isn't limited to just employer-employee associations, but in all types of relationships. There is even an example of it in God's Word.

In Matthew 13, Jesus traveled back to Nazareth where He grew up. The people from Nazareth knew Jesus from the time He was a child. They knew His family and His siblings. As Jesus instructed the people about His message, they were amazed at His wisdom.

"Where did this man get this wisdom and these deeds of power? Is not this the carpenter's son? Is not his mother called Mary? And are not his brothers James and Joseph and Simon and Judas? And are not all his sisters with us? Where then did this man get all this?" And they took offense at him. But Jesus said to them, "Prophets are not without honor except in their own country and in their own house" (Matthew 13:54-57).

At first these people were impressed with Jesus' knowledge, but the more they listened to His message, the more they reasoned in their own minds that He was simply a carpenter. Because these people knew Jesus as a small boy, their rigid perception excluded the possibility that He might be more than a common laborer. They refused to believe in His message. In Luke's account (4:16-30), the people were so angry with Jesus' message that "they got up, drove him out of the town, and led him to the brow of the hill on which their town was built, so that they might hurl him off the cliff. But he passed through the midst of them and went on his way." Clearly, Jesus didn't have their respect. Yet, because the Truth was in Him, He continued on. Luke 4:30 tells us that Jesus "went on his way." When we meet up with contempt, we are encouraged to continue on with the work God has for us.

The U.S. armed forces subscribe to the Familiarity Breeds Contempt model. It has long held the rule of non-fraternization between officers and enlisted personnel. When non approved fraternization behaviors exist, the resulting familiarity due to the forbidden association has the potential to compromise the integrity of authority, and can have a trickle affect down the chain of command. It then has the potential to compromise a team or unit's mission.[8] Other negative outcomes stemming from unapproved fraternization activities can include, among others, rank being taken advantage of, strong-arming actions, decline of morale, and the propensity of a skewed view of equality and fairness.[9]

To temper the perception of a hardline policy, officers and enlisted personnel can still become better acquainted–without compromising overall integrity and authority–in healthy and respectful ways, such as participating in a command team sport, working side-by-side in a worthy cause, participating in fundraisers, and hosting command family and children's events. These types of non-evasive relationships foster military camaraderie across all ranks and, in fact, can enhance respect for authority.

> **KEY POINT #3**
>
> In keeping our eyes fixed on Jesus, our posture should be a willingness to set aside fleshly urges to vindicate ourselves through equally dishonoring behaviors.

Psalm of Ascent 123 assures us of God's promise of mercy. Because of the scorn Jesus endured on our behalf, God is approachable. He is present in the midst of our deepest yearnings for relief from another's contempt.

Our role is to keep our eyes fixed on Jesus, patiently anticipating any movement of the Lord's hand, indicating His guidance. In doing so, our posture should be a willingness to set aside fleshly urges to vindicate ourselves through equally dishonoring behaviors.

In this promise of God's mercy, we may not find immediate relief as God's timetable is rarely in step with ours. Therefore, we must keep our gaze to heaven knowing our relief will come from the One enthroned. Only He knows the right course of deliverance and its perfect timing.

Prayer for Release of Contempt
Lord,

To You I lift up my eyes–You who are enthroned not only in heaven but also in my heart. Help me to not derive my worth based on what others say to me in verbal assaults. Remind me that my identity is in You and not in the perception of others. Protect my heart from becoming discouraged. Heal the wounds I have sustained from those who desire to beat me down with disrespectful words. Provide the strength needed so that I can resist emotional defeat.

Lord, I know that You are on my side (Psalm 118:6). And You are abundant in compassion (Lamentations 3:32). Even though others might want to speak ill of me or plan my demise, I am Yours, secure in Your arms of acceptance. In whatever rejection I may endure, may it serve to draw me closer to You.

Guard my heart from becoming bitter with thoughts of retaliating. Instead, give me the wisdom and guidance needed to navigate the disconcerting waters with God confidence. Uphold me with sufficient patience to wait for Your promise of relief. Amen.

Chapter Four Key Points
1. Repeated contemptuous remarks made by others should not deter us from courteously expressing our feelings towards God even when others are present.
2. In those times when we've had more than enough contempt–whether through unkind words or conveyed with an ugly

tone–our personal response is to settle our eyes upon Jesus and seek His mercy and His guidance.

3. In keeping our eyes fixed on Jesus, our posture should be a willingness to set aside fleshly urges to vindicate ourselves through equally dishonoring behaviors.

Reader's Reflections

1. If you've ever experienced a season of contempt, where did you fix your focus? How did you respond?

2. Are you easily deterred from sharing Jesus' message when you've been the target of disrespectful remarks? If so, how can Jesus' example change that?

Psalm of Strength

"Then they cried to the LORD in their trouble,
and he delivered them from their distress"
(Psalm 107:6).

* * *

PSALM OF ASCENT 124

* * *

[1] If it had not been the LORD who was on our
        side
        –let Israel now say–
[2] if it had not been the LORD,
          who was on our side,
        when our enemies attacked us,
[3] then they would have swallowed us up alive,
        when their anger was kindled against us;
[4] then the flood would have swept us away,
        the torrent would have gone over us;
[5] then over us would have gone
        The raging waters
[6] Blessed be the LORD,
        who has not given us
        as prey to their teeth.
[7] We have escaped like a bird
        from the snare of the fowlers;
        the snare is broken,
        and we have escaped
[8] Our help is in the name of the LORD,
        who made heaven and earth.

★ ★ ★ CHAPTER FIVE ★ ★ ★

IF IT HAD NOT BEEN
FOR THE Lord

Though I walk in the midst of trouble, you preserve
me against the wrath of my enemies; you stretched
out your hand, and your right hand delivers me.

Psalm 124:2

Have you ever experienced a close call of some kind–a car accident, or otherwise, and you knew without a doubt God prevented it? Or have you ever contemplated the number of times God stepped in front or behind you to safeguard you, but you were unaware of the danger?[1] This is the essence of what Psalm 124 addresses. Yet, there is more to this psalm than a mere acknowledgement that God came in at the eleventh hour and saved a people. There is a relationship here, between God and His children that needed His protection.

And God flanked them on every side. Even in the midst of their rebellion, God remained faithful and continuously looked upon the Israelites. These pilgrims were the apple of His eye (Psalm 17:8). God is for us today as well. However, our present-day assessment of what we believe God is capable of doing for us in times of great need or peril is

> **KEY POINT #1**
>
> Our present-day assessment of what we believe God is capable of doing for us in our time of need is inadequate. One way to better understand the depth of His care is by contemplating what would have taken place had it not been for the Lord.

inadequate. One way to arrive at a better understanding of the depth of His protection and concern is by contemplating what would have taken place had it not been for the Lord.

This psalm, again by David, is divided into two arrangements: (1) an appeal to declare God's rescue from four different calamities represented by metaphors, (vv. 1-5), and (2) exalting the name of the Lord.

David uses a group of metaphors to illustrate a vivid picture of Israel's enemies and their eventual escape. "When our enemies attacked us, then they would have swallowed us up alive" (vv. 2-3). God's people, portrayed as *prey* and their enemies as *vicious beasts* positioned themselves to devour them alive. Then in verses 4 and 5 David changes the metaphor. "When their anger was kindled against us; then the flood would have swept us away, the torrent would have gone over us; then over us would have gone the raging waters." Israel's enemies now symbolize a *flood* and a *torrent*. Like a natural disaster that comes suddenly and with overwhelming power, their enemies charged at them. They weren't just angry, they were enraged. And escape appeared impossible. Can you feel their utter desperation? Have you ever experienced a similar situation?

The job you perform in the military comes with inherent hazards. You don't know what the day will bring. America's enemies despise us and our presence ignites their anger, kindling a voracious appetite to swallow us. The Israelites were overwhelmed with threats of trouble, including destruction. We, too, can be consumed with overwhelming circumstances that, if we focus on them long enough, they will grow in our minds, blocking our hearts from trusting God to fight for us. At home, it is no different. The military family can also feel engulfed with its own share of debilitating challenges. You may not be fighting a physical enemy, but an enemy that nonetheless is real–Satan. In *Stepping Up: A Journey through the Psalms of Ascent*, author and Bible teacher, Beth Moore portrays Satan in his true light.

"Satan hates us because God loves us. He also hates us because we remind him of the position he lost. He was an anointed cherub. We are anointed children. He lost his place in heaven. Through Christ, we gained a place in heaven."[2]

Are you on deployment? Do the months away from home make you weary? Are you the military spouse struggling with burnout and problematic circumstances? Recognize these times as possible traps Satan hopes to ensnare you with. His mission is to kill, steal and destroy (John 10:10). He wants to kill your perseverance, steal your contentment, and destroy your peace. Don't be fooled by the cute depictions of a little red devil with his pitchfork. He means business. He'll stop at nothing to convince you in overwhelming circumstances and exhaustion that your service to your country is in vain, those months away on deployment or holding down the home front with children isn't honorable service. If Satan can get you to doubt the worthiness of your contribution, or the support you provide as the spouse, he has won half the battle. He will even take that pitchfork and use the words of other people to prick your heart into discouragement. An excessive attack of doubt has the potential to move your heart from the camp of contentment to the camp of dissatisfaction. Sitting in the camp of dissatisfaction positions you to shoot missiles of resentment at your spouse, the military organization, or others.

Don't allow Satan to bring division between you and your spouse during the long months of deployment. If Satan has gained ground in your thoughts, emotions, and actions, an awful pit grows in your soul as division grows in your heart. It causes your spirit to feel as far away as you physically are from each other. Instead, arm yourself with God's Word.

KEY POINT #2

An excessive attack of doubt has the potential to move your heart from the camp of contentment to the camp of dissatisfaction.

First Corinthians 15:58 offers us marching orders: "Be steadfast, immovable, always excelling in the work of the Lord, because you know that in the Lord your labor is not in vain." God runs His creation on a lean budget; nothing is thrown out as unusable. Even the emotional struggles we encounter in the often difficult military lifestyle are recycled back into our lives as learning lessons. Henry Ford, founder of the Ford Motor Company once said, "When everything seems to be going against you, remember that the airplane takes off against the wind, not with it."[3] We must see the difficult situations as a military member or family member from the perspective of what we endure contributes to the end result.

Our culture has a terrible nemesis that shows no signs of reversing. We want everything instantly. However, this is rarely God's way in the boot camp of life. Hebrews 12:1-2 says,

> Therefore, since we are surrounded by so great a cloud of witnesses, let us also lay aside every weight and the sin that clings so closely, and let us run with perseverance the race that is set before us, looking to Jesus the pioneer and perfecter of

our faith, who for the sake of the joy that was set before him endured the cross, disregarding its shame, and has taken his seat at the right hand of the throne of God.

Jesus kept His eye on the prize–the joy of securing salvation for all mankind–and now He is in the presence of His heavenly Father.

Likewise, God has given each of us our *particular* race–either as a military family or the military member, and we are to do two things with His help: (1) run the military obstacle course with excellence and patience, and (2) keep our eyes focused on Jesus.

As a military wife for seventeen years, I kept those two principles in the forefront of my mind. I didn't always succeed; I failed at times, but they became my benchmarks to motivate me to reach two rewards. The first reward I call my heart's reward, or my earthly reward–is homecoming day and getting that first glimpse of my husband, Ray, walking down the ship's brow, and (2) my heavenly reward–hearing from God one day, "Well done, my good and faithful servant." On those particularly hard days, such as anniversaries or the birthdays of our children, I reminded myself that this time of hard waiting will end. Our faith grows, not from our seasons of ease, but from our seasons of difficulties. After each of my husband's deployments, I not only gained a measure of self-confidence, but I grew in God-confidence–depending on Him, rather than on my passing emotions.

We must not forget that Jesus also suffered overwhelming struggles. Hebrews 2:18 says, "Because he himself was tested by what he suffered, he is able to help those who are being tested." He understands the unique trials and difficulties you face. He will not abandon those who diligently seek and depend on Him.

In verse 6, the metaphor used for Israel is a bird outwitted and snared by a hunter.[4] Israel's very existence hung in the balance under the Philistine threat. Yet, God was on Israel's side. Just as it seemed like it was curtains for them, God, in all His might delivered a way of escape. Even the Philistine army, as powerful as they were could not outmaneuver Israel's God.

The Lord Defends His People

David's portrayal of depicting his people as escaped birds conjures up several associations. Birds give us the feeling of freedom, or a lack of restraints. Here, our psalmist doesn't tell us what the way of escape was. David simply gives us revealing word pictures of how remarkable it had to be. "Blessed be the Lord, who has not given us as prey to their teeth." Joshua 23:10 reminds us of whose battle it really is. "It is the Lord your God who fights for you, as he promised you."

> **TODAY'S PEARL**
>
> "It is the Lord your God who fights for you" (Joshua 23:10).

In Praise for His Help

God defended His people. And they were not only relieved, but thankful. If you read verse 8 again, the tone of relief and gratitude is noticeable. Israel witnessed God's all-mighty deliverance and it called for exalting God. "O give thanks to the Lord, call on his name, make known his deeds among the peoples. Sing to him, sing praises to him, tell of all his wonderful works" (1 Chronicles 16:8-9).

The book of Psalms is filled with anthems of thanksgiving to God and His Word. Praising God is more than simply giving credit where credit is due–although that is part of praising God, but it is also a deeply personal gesture

> **KEY POINT #3**
>
> When we acknowledge God as our defender, we recognize His deliverance originates from His hand and all glory rightly belongs to Him.

of appreciation and recognizing God's significance and greatness in our lives. When we acknowledge God as our defender, we recognize His deliverance originates from His hand. As we grow to know His character and His ways, our appreciation for Him also grows. Psalm 96:4 says, "For great is the LORD, and greatly to be praised; he is to be revered above all gods." There are four essential action principles we can put into practice to show our thanks to God:

1. *Remembering* what God has done.
2. *Telling* others about it.
3. *Showing* God's glory to others
4. *Offering* gifts of self, time, and resources [5]

God is our Defender corporately and personally whether we are facing danger from our country's enemies, an unbearable family situation, difficult work circumstances, or from people whose hearts are bent against us, God is for us. We are also the apple of His eye and He is on our side. But why is it that our culture underestimates God's abilities to solve or move mightily in some of our most painful and challenging circumstances? We must learn to call on our Lord like David and his people did. There is no problem or circumstance too tough or too far gone for the Creator of heaven and earth. We need to trust Him to fight for us.

Psalm 124 looks into the troubles of history, the anxiety of personal conflict and emotional trauma.[6] But what the psalmist wants us to come away with is *who* it is that flanks us in the midst of trouble. Psalm 124 also offers us another perspective to ponder. How many situations are you aware of in which God delivered you? Now think for a moment about what *could* have happened if it had not been for the Lord.

It is Christ not culture that defines our lives.[7] It is the help we experience, not the hazards we risk, that shapes our days.[8] It is because of these events and others that gave the pilgrims a reason to traveled to Jerusalem to rejoice, proclaiming His wonderful work in their lives.

A Prayer of Praise to God, Our Defender

Lord,

As I grow to know You, the more I appreciate You. As the apple of Your eye (Psalm 17:8), You have kept me from being swallowed by the raging waters of overwhelming circumstances and from people who despise me. Out of immense care, You have made a way of escape, a way through to victory. You did not leave me defenseless. People may leave me, but You will never quit on me. And Your protection is limitless; it has no boundaries. Use any pain or suffering I endure to teach me spiritual lessons so that it makes me into a better servant for You. Let me be a praising person who never forgets what You have done, or will do, telling others so they will see Your mighty hand at work and praise Your name (Matthew 5:16).

Lord, show me the areas I am vulnerable to attacks by Satan so I can arm myself with Your Word. Continue to develop my level of trust in You so I remain firmly rooted in my faith. With Your defensive help, I will prevail over my enemy–Satan. Like You did for the Israelites, keep Your eye upon me. Because You were on their side, I can trust that You are for me, too. Amen.

Chapter Five Key Points

1. Our present-day assessment of what we believe God is capable of doing for us in our time of need is inadequate. One way to better understand the depth of His care is by

contemplating what would have taken place had it not been for the Lord.

2. An excessive attack of doubt has the potential to move your heart from the camp of contentment to the camp of dissatisfaction.

3. When we acknowledge God as our defender, we recognize His deliverance originates from His hand and all glory rightly belongs to Him.

Reader's Reflections

1. Has there ever been a situation where you felt like the Israelites did, as prey about to be devoured?

2. If God hadn't intervened in some way, what do you propose would have been the outcome?

3. Do you think there are any situations for which God will not defend us?

Psalm of Strength

"I call upon the LORD, who is worthy to be praised, so I shall be saved from my enemies"
(Psalm 18:3).

PSALM OF ASCENT 125

¹ Those who trust in the LORD are like
       Mount Zion, which cannot be moved,
       but abides forever.
² As the mountains surround Jerusalem, so
       the LORD surrounds his people, from this
       time on and forevermore.
³ For the scepter of wickedness shall not rest
       on the land allotted to the righteous,
       so that the righteous might not stretch
       out
       their hands to do wrong.
⁴ Do good, O LORD, to those who are good,
       and to those who are upright in their
       hearts.
⁵ But those who turn aside to their own
       crooked ways
       the LORD will lead away with evildoers.
       Peace be upon Israel!

GOD'S STRENGTH SURROUNDS ME

As the mountains surround Jerusalem,
so the Lord surrounds his people.
Psalm 125:2

n the summer of 2007, just after my daughter, Megan's, high school graduation, she was diagnosed with thyroid cancer. It couldn't have come at a worse time (Does cancer ever come at a convenient time?). She was preparing for her freshman year of college at Washington State University in Pullman, Washington, after successfully completing the multiple phases of the qualification process for a ROTC (Reserve Officer Training Corps) scholarship. In her senior year of high school, she received one of the ten spots in the program. Knowing she'd be getting down and dirty in the ROTC, I insisted she get her booster tetanus shot as hers had expired.

As it turned out, while at her appointment for the tetanus shot, her doctor did a neck scan with her fingers and found a suspiciously large lump. After a painful biopsy a week later, in which snippets of tissue were cut from her thyroid, the results came back–positive for cancer. Suddenly, her college enthusiasm melted and replaced by a fear of an unknown future. Everything came to a screeching halt. Because the test results came on the very day we were to move her to college, her father and I couldn't promise Megan that we'd still leave that same day, or that she would be going to college that fall. Even though all her things were packed in our camper, we had to step back and reassess things in light of her new medical situation.

Her dad, being the "*lets-get-it-done*" military man, immediately got busy on the phone. By 3:00 that same afternoon, he had found a cancer doctor in Pullman and discussed with him Megan's cancer diagnosis. The doctor stressed the urgency to get her in for surgery to remove the cancerous thyroid, but that it was likely she would also have to undergo radiation treatment. Not wanting to give up her college opportunity, she was optimistic that she could manage college and cancer at the same time. Even though she was turning nineteen and this is what Megan wanted, I wasn't convinced it was the best way to proceed.

After faxing the biopsy results to her new doctor and securing a surgery date for the following week which happened to be her first week of classes, my husband felt she would be in good hands. We left for the five hour drive to the small college town. Although we had things in place, the only unknown was what would become of her standing in the ROTC program. It was a prayerful week.

Because the cancer was extensive, the surgeon took Megan's entire thyroid and eleven lymph nodes. Thankfully, the cancer hadn't spread. Two days after her surgery she was allowed to leave the hospital. Back in her dorm room, my son, Lawrence helped us in getting her settled and comfortable, but I was still unsure we were doing the right thing. My heart was troubled that we had to leave later that day. She was still weak from surgery and unsteady on her feet. Having already missed her first week of classes, she was anxious to start, but she didn't seem well enough to begin classes in two days. Thinking about all that was ahead of her, it felt wrong to leave her at college to go through radiation therapy and mend herself without her family by her side. *Lord, I can't stay to take care of her. Would You give her the strength she needs to get well enough to stay in school?* I prayed. As expected, she lost her full scholarship as well as her position in the ROTC program.

By 4:00pm it was time to head back home. We went over the doctor's notes, her medication schedule and the following week's doctor's appointments one last time. Ray gave her a big bear hug and told her to take one day at a time, and simply to do her best in school. As I picked up my purse, my eyes filled up with tears as the dreaded moment came. I leaned over the edge of her bed, hugged her gently, and told her I loved her and that we'd be calling her daily. Once out in the dorm hallway, the distress I felt at leaving her ill rushed to the surface and the tears just spilled over. My husband didn't say anything; he simply reached over and took my hand, and the three of us walked back to our car.

Not long after surgery she began radiation treatment. As warned by her doctor, the extreme fatigue and nausea from the radiation was debilitating; her fatigue was nothing like she'd ever experienced before. The first four months were brutal. Most days she mustard enough strength to make it to her classes, but walking the campus' hilly terrain left her physically exhausted, laboring for every breath. She simply didn't have enough strength to attend her afternoon classes.

She collapsed in bed stripped of any energy reserves for completing her homework.

Because the body needs energy to heal during radiation therapy, enough calorie and protein intake is critical. Megan was required to be on a special diet while undergoing radiation therapy, but dorm living wasn't conducive to a medically mandated diet. She struggled to get adequate nutrition. Worried, I offered to come and stay with her a week at a time, attend her classes, record the lectures, and help her with her special diet, but she assured me that her boyfriend, Josh, now her husband, was able to drive over several times a month to see her and help with making meals. Even though they had only met just six months prior, it eased my mind to know she wasn't alone.

Relieved that her rounds of radiation was over with no cancer cells detected, she began taking thyroid medication, of which she'd be on the rest of her life. By Christmas she was starting to feel stronger even though her face still looked pale. Thankfully, she continued to improve.

Early into her second semester, with her father's encouragement, she decided to pursue getting her ROTC scholarship reinstated; however, she had to re-qualify both medically and physically. Still too weak, she failed the first two attempts. But, by late spring, on her third attempt, she passed. Because she missed most of the training that first year, she had to work extra hard to catch up with her fellow cadets. After a grueling first year of college, this victory put a smile back into her heart. Her grades were nothing stellar, squeaking by with a D average. Disappointed, we encouraged her that there would be time later to rebound academically.

Four years later and still cancer free, with a 3.2 gpa, we witnessed with inexpressible joy and thanksgiving, our daughter's Army commissioning as a second lieutenant. As the tradition goes, her dad, being the noncommissioned officer, had the proud honor of giving his

---

KEY POINT #1

God's past help increases our trust in Him, becoming the foundation for our strength.

---

daughter her first salute during the ceremony. The following day she graduated with her degree in Criminal Justice.

If it had not been the Lord who prompted me to insist she get her tetanus shot updated, her cancer would of gone undetected. As her mother, I could only fathom what the alternative outcome might have been. Because God's love protects, I believe He intervened in Megan's life.

Psalm of Ascent 125 is a song of trust. In chapter five we looked at how God's care defends His people. In this chapter, we'll unpack the meaning of the metaphors of how His love protects. At its most basic level, God loved these pilgrims because He created them. Even with their inconsistent faith, their tendency to drift towards idol worship, and their frequent confrontations with their enemies, God was about His work on their behalf–proving He was mightier than any human ruler.

Psalm 125:1 says: "Those who trust in the LORD are like Mount Zion, which cannot be moved, but abides forever." Mount Zion also appears in 2 Samuel 5:7: "Nevertheless, David took the stronghold of Zion, which is now the city of David." The Jebusites, a Canaanite tribe that had never been expelled from the land, had control of Mount Zion.[1] From their perspective, they had a military advantage and even boasted of their security behind the impregnable walls of Jerusalem.[2] David, being a strong military strategist, found a way to overthrow the Jebusite's control by gaining access of the city through the water tunnel, seizing control of the mount.[3] Jerusalem eventually became known as Mount Zion. Made of solid rock, it exudes stability. Mount Zion is a picture of strength.

The psalmist made a comparison. When God's people place their trust in the Lord they are like Mount Zion, strong and steady. If our spiritual tanks are full by the nourishment of God's Word, His strength will surround us protecting us from being moved off our foundations. God's past help reinforces our trust in Him for current troubles. It doesn't matter what it is–your family, your city, your business or your heart–if God is the nucleus, His strength establishes us. The roots of God's strength sink deep. Having spiritual strength is necessary if we want to do more than just cope with the military life. The struggles and the unique circumstances of military personnel and their families is unlike civilian life. Lengthy war campaigns, missions, and deployments can erode your sense of control and well-being if not balanced with daily spiritual nurture. War can also cloud our perception about the condition of our world. It can amplify feelings that life has no meaning or purpose. Consistent spiritual nourishment for Christian military members and their families balances the scales, assuring us that God is still on the throne and still in control, despite how things look from our perspective.

Psalm 46:1 describes the Source of our strength: "God is our refuge and strength, a very present help in trouble." It doesn't say that God is our refuge and strength *only* when He feels like it. Whether on the battlefield of war or the battlefield of life, God

> **KEY POINT #2**
>
> Whether on the battlefield of war or the battlefield of life, God freely surrounds His children. Whether or not He allows trouble to touch our lives, God is still present.

freely surrounds His children. Whether or not He allows trouble to touch our lives, God is still present. We must continue to trust and take Him at His Word.

In L.B. Cowman's devotional book, *Streams in the Desert*, is a commentary by R. Leighton. It reveals a harsh reality that leaves a person vulnerable.

"What is it that causes people to shake like leaves today at the first hint of danger? It is simply the lack of God living in their soul, and having the world in their hearts instead."[4]

His Love Protects

Psalm 125:2 tells us, "As the mountains surround Jerusalem, so the LORD surrounds his people, from this time on and forevermore." Mount Zion sits lower than the surrounding hills.[5] This provides an impression that a wall surrounds Jerusalem.[6] Just as the wall surrounds the city, protecting it, God's love surrounds His people protecting them.[7] Psalm 34:7 also portrays God as settling around those who show respect and devotion to Him. "The angel of the LORD encamps around those who fear him, and delivers them." God knows His servants completely and He promises to position Himself close.

> ### TODAY'S PEARL
>
> "You hem me in, behind and before, and lay your hand upon me" (Psalm 139:5).

Psalm 139:5 became my prayer for my daughter, Megan. Each time she returned home from college, she traveled over the Cascade Mountains. During the winter months, driving at times became treacherous with the threat of avalanches. In the New King James Bible, the word **hedge** is used in place of hem. Either way, His presence guides, loves, and protects. Likewise, the opposite is true. There is nowhere we can flee to be outside of His parameters of love. Romans 8:35 says, "Who will separate us from the love of Christ? Will hardship, or distress, or persecution, or famine, or nakedness, or peril, or sword?" No, it is not possible to be outside of His love.

Equally true, there is nothing we can do to cause Him to pull His love from us.

Our psalmist in verse 3 takes us into a new direction of thinking about God's protective love. In the previous verses, God's strength surrounds His people and His love protects from enemies *outside* of the city, but what about those living within their allotted land? What about God's children living *inside* the city in the midst of an ungodly ruler? Verse 3 says, "For the scepter of wickedness shall not rest on the land allotted to the righteous." A scepter is a rod or a staff, symbolizing authority. The psalmist is saying here that those who are in authority, who rule with an evil hand over God's people in their own land, will not settle the land indefinitely because it belongs to His people.[8] God is consistent with this claim.

Recall in chapter one where God ordered Joshua to destroy those nations who worshipped idols and engaged in evil behavior because He knew His children would be enticed to participate. Even though Joshua failed in that area, God's goal was to protect them from being corrupted by sin. Here again, in Psalm 125, out of His love He protected His pilgrims "so that the righteous might not stretch out their hands to do wrong." God was not about to let evil people settle forever on the land reserved for His righteous ones and watch them fall into heathen practices.

Military members who serve or have served in war zones abroad not only fight physical enemies, but also those who ruled their people with an evil spirit such as Hitler and former Iraq's president Saddam Hussein. Nations and rulers continue to rise and fall as we have seen in recent years in the Middle East. God's promise is that He won't allow ungodly people to rule forever over those with upright hearts.[9] He will allow the wicked to stumble and they will reap the consequences of the evil they themselves manifested. He, at a time only He determines, will execute His judgment and eradicate those with a scepter of evil.

For believers our comfort is this: If evil touches the lives of our brothers and sisters in Christ who serve our country, God's Word assures us that not only is God present with them, (Psalm 23:4) but that God immediately brings them to their heavenly home (2 Corinthians 5:8).

The final section of this psalm reveals God's moral nature. Just as God will oppose those who partake of evil and embrace dishonest ways, it is both refreshing and encouraging to know that He will also reward His faithful ones. "Do good, O LORD, to those who are good, and to those who are upright in their hearts. But those who turn aside to their own crooked ways the LORD will lead away with evildoers. Peace be upon Israel!" Israel will see peace when God balances the scales with His justice.

This sixth song of ascent sang by the pilgrims is a testament to God's strength and protection over the godly. As they walked, they declared His power over the wicked. They concluded their song with a prayer that God would bless them, curse the wicked, and bring peace to Israel.

Prayer to Trust

Lord,

I know that it requires trust in You to be as immoveable like Mount Zion. It is my heart's desire to trust in You even in difficult circumstances and when I don't know what the outcome will be. Increase my faith so that it will translate into a strength that will resist trembling and fear. Teach me to draw strength from You so that I am empowered for every battle I encounter. You are my Rock, my Zion, and I am thankful that Your love is so complete that it is like the mountains that surround Jerusalem–protecting her, protecting me. Although I can't fathom Your magnificence, I am grateful that Your love is a vehicle of protection.

Lord, You are a just God and You will bring justice to those who hold the scepter of wickedness (Psalm 125:3) and You will not withhold Your good to those who are godly (Psalm 125:4). To the faint and powerless, You bless with strength (Isaiah 40:29). Thank You for being my Source of strength. Help me to stand on Your promises so I can have victory today. Thank You, Lord, that Your eye is on those who revere You (Psalm 33:18). Amen.

Chapter Six Key Points

1. God's past help increases our trust in Him, becoming the foundation for our strength.
2. Whether on the battlefield of war or the battlefield of life, God freely surrounds His children with fortress-like strength.

Reader's Reflections

1. Is there an experience in your life or in the lives of your family in which God's love protected you or them from danger, physically, health wise, monetarily, or in some other way?
2. Has there ever been a time in which God's past help made a significant different in your trust of God?

Psalm of Strength

"Those who love me, I will deliver;
I will protect those who know my name"
(Psalm 91:14).

PSALM OF ASCENT 126

[1] When the Lᴏʀᴅ restored the fortunes of
    Zion,we were like those who dream.
[2] Then our mouth was filled with laughter,
    and our tongue with shouts of joy;
    then it was said among the nations,
      "The Lᴏʀᴅ has done great things for them."
[3] The Lᴏʀᴅ has done great things for us,
    and we rejoiced.
[4] Restore our fortunes, O Lᴏʀᴅ,
    like the watercourses in the Negeb.
[5] May those who sow in tears
    reap with shouts of joy.
[6] Those who go out weeping,
    bearing the seed for sowing,
    shall come home with shouts of joy,
    carrying their sheaves.

REMEMBERING GOOD TIMES, BUT ON HOLD FOR MORE

The LORD has done great things for them.

Psalm 126:2

as this year been especially difficult? Was it a deployment year, or a year filled with numerous training missions with a demanding schedule? Or was it a year with financial worries, health issues, or concerns over children? It's no surprise that some years the trials come one season after another with little or no peace in between.

Early in our marriage and in my husband's military career, I experienced a very long season without peace. I struggled with infertility. With my husband, Ray, underway at sea more than he was home, the years swiftly rolled by. When he was home we resumed infertility treatments, but to no avail. In our sixth year, my spirits hit rock bottom. I was turning thirty-five years old and a sense of loss was heavy on my heart. Depressed, I cried out to God many times, asking, "How long, Lord? How much longer until this heartache goes away?" It seemed as if I was living between two realms–between a time filled with fond memories of good experiences, and another time waiting for good times to return again. A new kind of longing settled into my heart–a longing to laugh again. Can you relate? Do you feel as though you're living between the times–remembering the good times, but on hold for more?

Psalm 126 describes this period of living between two realms. It says: "When the Lord restored the fortunes of Zion, we were like those who dream" (v. 1).The psalmist is rejoicing over an important event. Many scholars believe this psalm was written during the time period following the release of the Israelites from their captivity from Babylon. Because the people had been waiting for the moment of freedom for many years, they were utterly astonished, perhaps questioning whether it was really happening. God did something so wonderful it seemed like a dream. The temperament of this psalm reflects the elation these pilgrims felt in the moment of new found liberty. "Then our mouth was filled with laughter, and our tongue with shouts of joy." In the second half of verse 2, "then it was said among the nations, 'The Lord has done great things for them.'" "The Lord has done great things for us, and we rejoiced.'" As servants of God, the pilgrims proclaimed their testimonies of events such as this one to all the nations, giving the glory to Yahweh.

History tells us that King Cyrus allowed different groups of exiles, including the Jews, to return to their homelands.[1] However, his gesture was not all selfless; it also had a military component-in *his* favor. By releasing the exiles, he hoped to win their loyalty and thus provide buffer zones around the borders of his empire.[2] Interestingly, Isaiah prophesied that a man named Cyrus would issue a pronouncement allowing the Israelites to return to their homeland. (see Isaiah 44:28; 45:1). King Cyrus wasn't a servant of Israel's God, but he did show compassion and kindness to the captives. Ezra 1:1 says that God "stirred up the spirit of King Cyrus of Persia." God can use whatever instrument He deems necessary to bring about His desired will. Here we see Him using this king with a benevolent heart to bring His chosen people out of captivity.

In verse 4, the psalmist shifts the focus of the psalm from remembering God's past mercies upon His people to lifting up a prayer request. Our pilgrims, as they traveled to and from Jerusalem reflected on a period of history when God turned the tide of their ancestor's circumstances. They concluded that only something that good had to be from God. This is the in-between times that James Limburg describes: "Psalm 126 comes from a people who are living between the times, between a good time remembered and another good time hoped for."[3]

What about you? Can you think of an event that seemed too good to be true, but it was? For me, it was the day I learned I was finally pregnant. After six disappointing years of secondary infertility, I was exhausted. The emotional roller coaster month after month and the varying treatment plans, intensified the anxiety and the heaviness on my heart. By the sixth year, my depressed disposition was affecting not only myself and my husband, but our marriage, too. Deep down I knew it was time to stop. It had all became too much–I called it quits. I threw up the white surrender flag and gave my fight with infertility to the Lord. It was a day-by-day commitment, some days harder than others. I still cried. I still prayed, but I was weary from it and found myself praying for something else instead–my joy to be restored.

Several months passed and the incredible happened; I was expecting! Even Ray, when he called home from the ship was hopeful, but skeptical. Later that year, our son, Lawrence was born. In those six years of waiting and praying, my prayerful tears became the fertile soil to receive the seed for God's harvest. I don't know why God put seven years between my children, but perhaps to teach me about trusting and waiting on Him rather than striving in my own strength, or to be a testimony and a source of encouragement to other women experiencing infertility. Nothing strengthens our faith more than when we recall former instances of how God ended a season of captivity, or a period of dry, thirsty, and disappointing times, and ushered in occasions of blessings. It provides genuine

---

KEY POINT #1

Nothing strengthens our faith more than when we recall former instances of how God ended a season of captivity, or a period of dry, thirsty, and disappointing times and ushered in occasions of blessings.

---

evidence to Psalm 27:13-14 which says, "I believe that I shall see the goodness of the LORD in the land of the living. Wait for the LORD; be strong, and let your heart take courage; wait for the LORD!"

From Seed to Sheaves

It is in the second three verses that the psalmist uses two metaphors to emphasize God bringing about a fresh season of restored circumstances. The first one is the Negeb metaphor. "Restore our fortunes, O LORD, like the watercourses in the Negeb." If God can end a season of drought and provide a year of abundant crops on the normally dry water beds of the region of Negeb, He is fully able to fill our weary spirits with joy by doing something remarkable for us.

Ephesisans 3:20 is a testament to what God can do beyond what we think is possible. It says, "Now to him who by the power at work within us is able to accomplish abundantly far more than all we can ask or imagine." God, who is without limits, is the ultimate Source for creativity, and He still desires to bless His children with events that astonish us. Our posture should be one of hopeful expectation while He has us in the waiting room. A farmer who plants seed in his fields must wait for it to sprout, grow, and then mature, until the day of harvest. The farmer knows the growth comes from the Lord, but if we're like a farmer who becomes impatient for the growth to come and tills up the soil, believing no harvest will ever come, we've given up on the seed, cutting off the blessing God had for us. This isn't to say that our harvest will come in a relatively short period of time. In fact, a harvest of blessing can sometimes mean a lifetime of long-suffering (years of patient waiting).

Some of us have deep thorns of affliction, requiring faithful prayer, supported by years of sowing the seed of God's Word into the situation. We can take comfort in knowing that God will not permit us to go through a period of suffering without a reason. If we remain steadfast, never giving up on God, trusting in His timing, His plan, and His Word, He is faithful to bring in the harvest. One note of precaution: God may bring about a different kind of harvest than what we are expecting. He may be sending a harvest of blessings, but through a different means or channel. If that is the case, trust Him that He knows what's best.

Does this psalm describe your circumstances right now? Maybe you've reflected on some wonderful things God has done for you in the past, but it has been such a long season of dry and disheartened circumstances that you long to see God bless you with something wonderful again?

Those taken into captivity to Babylon were carried away in tears, signaling the start of their sorrow spanning seventy years.

TODAY'S PEARL

"Now to him who by the power at work within us is able to accomplish abundantly far more than all we can ask or imagine" (Ephesians 3:20).

Their tears became the seeds for a future harvest of joy that would be theirs later. In fact, this is the meaning of the second metaphor: "May those who sow in tears reap with shouts of joy" (v.6). At the end of their captivity, God did the extraordinary and ended their bondage, producing a new season of joy. His capacity for restoring life is beyond our understanding.[4] He is able to bring joy out of the difficult and deadest of places and seasons. Our complete restoration may not be in this life–but it will happen.[5] God is just. He will not only restore whatever we have lost unjustly, but he will give us more than we can imagine as we live with him in eternity.[6] We only need to trust God with all we don't understand and hold tightly to our faith.

KEY POINT #2

God's capacity for restoring life is beyond our understanding. He is able to bring joy out of the difficult places and seasons.

I liken the first half of verse 5 to the day we send our sailor, soldier, airman, or marine off on deployment. If you're a Navy wife like I was, you made that dreaded drive to the pier, not wanting to let go of your spouse, but at the same time needing to pull away so you can move past that terrible ache in your heart. And if the scheduled ship's deployment lands on a dark, rainy morning, typical of a winter day in the Pacific Northwest, the streaks of rain across the belly of the warship resemble the many tear-streaked faces of dedicated spouses and children left behind. Your tears, when prayerfully sowed, are the seeds for your future harvest. "Those who go out weeping, bearing the seed for sowing, shall come home with shouts of joy, carrying their sheaves." But what does "carrying their sheaves" mean? Sheaves are bundles of wheat tied together as it is gathered. Bringing in the sheaves means bringing in the harvest. During the long months of deployment, life can get hard, lonely, and bittersweet. Thankfully, hard times do end as do deployments. Likewise, for as surely as seed is planted, there is a harvest, as long as God's Word is sowed into these challenging circumstances.

KEY POINT #3

For as surely as seed is planted, there is a harvest, as long as God's Word is sowed into these challenging circumstances.

On homecoming day you trade those tears of patient waiting and difficult days for shouts of joy. There is nothing this side of heaven, after your wedding day and the birth of your children, so dear to you as waiting pier-side scanning the thousands of sailors descending the ship's brow when you suddenly spot your husband, looking ever so handsome in his freshly pressed uniform. And for the waiting husband, longing to feel your wife's soft embrace, to have the love of your life home safe is to know a blissful moment. Your heart swells with pride knowing that behind your husband or wife, there you are standing beside him or her in support.

Finally home, God has ended that "good time remembered." You and your family can now, with joy move to the other side of James Limburg's quote to "another good time hoped for." Long-awaited military homecomings are your sheaves of the harvest.

Prayer for a Future Harvest

Lord,

You are our confident expectation. And only by faith in You can we find genuine joy. Your joy is what satisfies my soul. Help me to see that my circumstances, however disappointing, can be turned into fertile ground. The tears I shed can be the seeds for a future harvest. You have promised me a future and a hope, but a long season of disappointment can block me from experiencing emotional and spiritual development, as well as Your joy. Help me to move past the crushing disappointment of (insert your season of disappointment here)so that I can see "the goodness of the LORD in the land of the living" (Psalm 27:13). Strengthen my heart to wait for You so I can reap the benefit of patiently waiting, while sowing the tears of my circumstances into Your Word.

Lord, I'm living between the times–between a good time remembered and a good time still waiting for. I pray that You would work out my difficult circumstances according to Your purposes and Your will, so that I and those I love can experience that good time hoped for in the future. Help me to be mindful of my brethren who may also still be in difficult places in their lives, to be as the watercourses of the Negeb. Let me bring refreshment and encouragement to their weary hearts that You will indeed bring them through a hard situation, so they, too, can carry their sheaves of the harvest.

Lord, I know that this life will bring additional challenges and disappointments. "I will bless you as long as I live; I will lift up my hands and call on your name" (Psalm 63:4). I will cling to You and my faith. Let me not forget what You did for Israel, knowing You won't leave me in my disappointing circumstances. Amen.

Chapter Seven Key Points

1. Nothing strengthen our faith more than when we recall former instances of how God ended a season of captivity, or a period of dry, thirsty, and disappointing times and ushered in occasions of blessings.

2. God's capacity for restoring life is beyond our understanding. He is able to bring joy out of the difficult places and seasons.

3. For as surely as seed is planted, there is a harvest, as long as God's Word is sowed into these challenging circumstances.

Reader's Reflections

1. Have you ever experienced something like the Israelites did–a dramatic work of God that seemed too good to be true, but was? If so, what was it?

2. On a scale of 1 to 10, with 10 being the most difficult, how hard is it for you to remain patient for God to turn the tide of your circumstances? Are you prone to giving up too soon? If so, what do you need to change in order to allow God to bring you through to attain "another good time hoped for"?

3. If you are not in a difficult place right now, what are you looking forward to seeing God do for you in the future?

Psalm of Strength

"Blessed be the Lord, who daily bears us up"

(Psalm 68:19).

PSALM OF ASCENT 127

[1] Unless the Lord builds the house,
    those who build it labor in vain.
    Unless the Lord guards the city,
    the guard keeps watch in vain.
[2] It is in vain that you rise up early
    and go late to rest,
    eating the bread of anxious toil;
    for he gives sleep to his beloved.
[3] Sons are indeed a heritage from the Lord,
    the fruit of the womb a reward.
[4] Like arrows in the hand of a warrior
    are the sons of one's youth.
[5] Happy is the man who has
    his quiver full of them.
    He shall not be put to shame
    when he speaks with his enemies
    in the gate.

UNLESS THE Lord BUILDS

Unless the Lord builds the house,
those who build it labor in vain.
Psalm 127:1

King Solomon had everything our modern world today hungers after: wisdom, power, success, honor, wealth, and pleasure. Yet none of them gave him true satisfaction. In the book of Ecclesiastes, Solomon reveals what he discovered as a result of his experiences–that a life without God lacked enjoyment, fulfillment, and meaning. Knowing his wealth and possessions were fleeting, he chose what was lasting–pursuing a life that pleased God. The by-products of this pursuit satisfied his feelings of longing and emptiness. Solomon's wisdom is still applicable today. In a world that tries to mask the truth in shades of gray, this one thing remains: Without God, all our pursuits are futile. This Song of Ascent, written by Solomon, was near and dear to the pilgrims' hearts as they considered its wisdom.

Pursuing a life that pleases God begins with the foundation of our homes. "According to the grace of God given to me, like a skilled master builder I laid a foundation, and someone else is building on it. Each builder must choose with care how to build on it. For no one can lay any foundation other than the one that has been laid; that foundation is Jesus Christ" (1 Corinthians 3:10).

If we want our military homes to be resilient in the face of storms, Christ must be its foundation (v.1). Jesus laid the groundwork and it is up to us to build on it. This is equally true of our cities, or in the broader sense, our country. Whether we are building a career, business, relationships, a home, or protecting our country, these endeavors are futile unless God is in them. God longs to be involved in the development and design phase of your home. The President of the United States may be your commander-in-chief, but Uncle Sam isn't the foreman on the building of your home or life.

KEY POINT #1

Whether we are building a career, business, relationships, a home, or protecting our country, these endeavors are futile unless God is in them.

Furthermore, Psalm 127 also applies to the plans that we make and the children we birth. Walter C. Kaiser, Jr., in his book, *The Journey Isn't Over,* states, "In order to appreciate fully the depth of this psalm, we must first realize that 'builds the house' (v.1) does not simply refer to the material construction of buildings. It refers to everything that goes on in connection with life in the home."[1] Apart from an abiding life in Christ, our tendency is to strive in our own efforts to lay foundations of our own design. Society teaches the necessity of careful planning if we want to see our plans to fruition. In our humanity, we work hard believing this guarantees the success of our plans, yet we have not consulted the Lord. Knowing whether our plans are pleasing to Him or not, is part of doing our homework. If God isn't in the equation, our striving is meaningless. We won't be producing spiritual fruit.

Proverbs 16:9 says: "The human mind plans the way, but the LORD directs the steps." After all, it is God who determines how successful the work of our hands will be.

King David made the mistake of conjuring up his own plans without first running his proposal by God. After building his own house, David told the prophet Nathan, "See now, I am living in a house of cedar, but the ark of God stays in a tent." Nathan replies, "Go, do all that you have in mind; for the LORD is with you" (2 Samuel 7:2-3). God knew what plans David had in his heart (1 Chronicles 28:9). It didn't seem right to David that he had a fine house to live in, but the Ark of the Covenant sat in a tent. His plan included building a temple for God. Yet, God didn't sign off on David's plan. That night God told Nathan what to tell David concerning his plans to build God a temple.

When your days are fulfilled and you lie down with your ancestors, I will raise up your offspring after you, who shall come forth from your body, and I will establish his kingdom. He shall build a house for my name, and I will establish the throne of his kingdom forever (2 Samuel 7:12-13).

It wasn't that David's request was wrong. He was just the wrong person for the job. God was looking down the road, to the reign of David's son, Solomon, for building the temple. First Chronicles 28:19

supports godly planning. "All this, in writing at the LORD's direction, he made clear to me[David]–the plan of all the works." God laid out the plans for the building of His temple, then gave them to David who very well could have been the scribe.[2] And later, when Solomon was king of Israel, the temple was built according to God's written instructions. So, what kind of materials are we to use in the building of our homes?

In Isaiah 28:16, Jesus is referred to as the stone for a foundation. "See, I am laying in Zion a foundation stone, a tested stone, a precious cornerstone, a sure foundation." Jesus is the cornerstone– our sure foundation. The concept of a cornerstone gets it meaning when setting the first stone in place for a building project. This stone determines where the remaining stones will go. The walls are then placed on either side of the cornerstone, and it is the cornerstone that joins them both and furnishes the strength to the overall project. Just as it takes the right materials to construct a house, we also must use the right materials to build our godly homes and lives.

First Corinthians 3:12 gives us a list of building materials. "Now if anyone builds on the foundation with gold, silver, precious stones, wood, hay, straw–the work of each builder will become visible, for the Day will disclose it, because it will be revealed with fire, and the fire will test what sort of work each has done." Choosing godly building materials must be intentional for God to keep us on the path to a godly life and meaningful work.

Wood, Hay, and Straw

When studying the above-listed materials, look at them as two categories: perishable and imperishable–wood, hay, and straw are perishable; they burn up quickly. Gold, silver, and precious stones are imperishable–materials which remain established when tested, and represent good materials for building a home and a godly life. If Jesus is the cornerstone, a sure foundation, then we are the *living stones* (1 Peter 2:5) and our purpose is to build on God's spiritual undertakings. If God is not in what we are trying to build, we are choosing wood, hay, and straw as our building materials. These inferior materials ultimately damage Christ's foundation. Examples of building with inferior materials are: seeking wealth over the kingdom of God, possessing power instead of allowing the Lord to possess our hearts, and excessive self-interest and self-service over a heart of serving others. Of course there are others, but these types of building materials create cracks in our foundations, weakening the whole structure. And if we have children, we are passing along inferior building materials with which to build their homes. A family without God can never experience the spiritual bond God brings to relationships.[3]

In an online article called, "Works: Purified or Fried" by Keith Krell he tells this story:

> A wealthy woman died one day and went to heaven. An angel then took her to her heavenly abode, which was a plain old ordinary building. Right next door to her was her gardener who had a palatial mansion. She said, "How did my gardener get a mansion and I get a plain old ordinary building?" The angel then said, "Well, we only build with the materials you send us." If you're sending to heaven junk, junk is then what God uses. He uses only what you send Him!"[4]

Gold, Silver, and Precious Stones

Jesus was passionate about His instructions on how to build a strong and resilient home. In Matthew 7:24-25 He taught, "Everyone then who hears these words of mine and acts on them will be like a wise man who built his house on rock: and the rain descended, the floods came, and the winds blew and beat on that house; and it did not fall, for it was founded on the rock." Christ is our Rock and when we build on that Rock He not only calls us wise and says our homes will pass coming judgment, but it means we are fortifying our homes with toughness and resilience, necessary components in the fabric of an established military home. None of us in military families want

KEY POINT #2

It is paramount that we consider what materials we're using to build on our foundations for understanding the consequences of ignoring God's house-building instructions.

our homes or our lives to become like a house of cards, crumbling around our feet because of using inferior building materials. It is paramount that we consider what materials we're using to build upon our foundations for understanding the consequences of ignoring God's house-building instructions.

On the contrary, if God is in what we are building, the house built on rock embodies a life founded on a proper relationship to Christ.[5] Some examples of building with gold, silver and precious stones are: having a servant's heart, daily seeking and abiding in Christ, pursuing the things of God, and exhibiting a godly lifestyle that reflects the inward reality of Christ. In laboring to build your home and in the work you do in the military, these duties are performed trusting God for the results. The military may not mirror Christlikeness, yet God is at work within it. He uses godly military members—soldiers, sailors, marines, chaplains, corpsmen, platoon leaders, and others to further His kingdom work. "Unless the LORD guards the city, [or country] the guard keeps watch in vain"(v.1). Your military duties may seem routine, but when you perform your tasks as an act of service to God, combined with praying for your country and its leaders, and for God's guiding hand in all its affairs, you are procuring God to guard over and establish it. Any country, including America, that neglects or even rejects God will eventually incur severe consequences.

In verse 2, Solomon's wisdom is relevant today. "It is in vain that you rise up early and go late to rest, eating the bread of anxious toil; for he gives sleep to his beloved." Working till the point of exhaustion and going to bed late, only to rise early to start in again, is a meaningless existence. God created times for rest and times for work. If we are living with an anxious heart, worried about many things rest will be elusive. Beth Moore in her study, *Stepping Up:A Journey through the Psalms of Ascent,* has a fitting equation for this verse. "Godless labor + little sleep = a futile expenditure of energy."[6]

A Quiver Full of Blessings

Solomon turns his focus from building a godly home and life to God's gift of adding children to the home. "Sons are indeed a heritage from the LORD, the fruit of the womb a reward" (v. 3). The word *heritage* means "something transmitted by or acquired from a predecessor, a legacy, or inheritance."[7] According to God's Word, children are a heritage from God, a reward, a

KEY POINT #3

God has tasked you with the job of aiming your children towards a relationship with Christ.

blessing. Even though verse 3 refers to sons, daughters are included in this heritage. Parents of many children were regarded as a symbol of strength.[8] Having lots of hands working in the fields increased a farmers productivity.[9] Sons were also expected to defend the family and protect the home against enemy attacks. In verse 4, Solomon compares children to arrows: "Like arrows in the hand of a warrior are the sons of one's youth." Whether you have one child or several, God has tasked you with the job of aiming your children towards a relationship with Christ.

The last verse of this psalm is a tribute to the father who has many sons. "Happy is the man who has his quiver full of them" (v.5). A quiver is a case for carrying arrows. Solomon's use of the metaphor "*a quiver full of them*" represents a father with many sons. "He shall not be put to shame when he speaks with his enemies in the gate"(v. 5). In chapter three you read that in cases where a decision of the court couldn't be determined, the case was referred to the high priest. This is where a father who had many sons had an advantage in court. If a father had a case pending at the gate (court), his sons became his advocates.[10] They testified on their father's behalf. A father with several sons would be hard for an enemy to intimidate. Finally, the father with many sons is a well-respected man in his home town.

For my sisters in Christ, don't be discouraged by the favor sons had in ancient times. Remember, God used great women of faith such as Deborah, Esther, Ruth, Rahab, and others to minister to you and me today. And whether you have all sons or all daughters, or a mixture of the two, your children are today's arrows. As you and I age, they become our advocates. Proverbs 17:6 says, "Grandchildren are the crown of the aged, and the glory of children is their parents." With Christ as our foundation, we must invest in what God has established for us in order to leave our children a legacy of faith with good building materials. Since we know there is a day coming (1 Corinthians 3:12) in which God will evaluate all that we did in this life, we have to ensure we're choosing building materials that have eternal value instead of reaping sorrow from vain toil.

Prayer for Our Home and Children

Lord,

I know that a life without You is a life without meaning, and all my toil is rubbish. Unless I invite You into what I'm trying to do, my plans won't have Your blessing. Today, I ask You to be at the center of my life's goals, plans, career decisions and desires. This includes the lives of my family as well. Direct all my steps and make me sensitive to Your leading (Psalm 25:4). Help my husband (wife) and I to be in agreement about the plans we make. Give us hearts to seek those things which are above (Colossians 3:1) where Christ is seated, and enable us to put You first in our home. Help us to be mindful of what we choose to bring into our home. Teach us to build our home and lives with gold, silver, and precious stones–good building materials that make our home resilient to the stresses of the military lifestyle. Bring godly people into our lives to minister to us as parents. And give us discernment in spiritual matters that builds on Christ's foundation. Strengthen us in our resolve to keep You as the head of our home. Amen.

Chapter Eight Key Points

1. Whether we are building a career, business, relationships, a home, or protecting our country, these endeavors are futile unless God is in them.

2. It is paramount that we consider what materials we're using to build on our foundations for understanding the consequences of ignoring God's house-building instructions.

3. God has tasked you with the job of aiming your children towards a relationship with Christ.

Reader's Reflections

1. What types of challenges does the military lifestyle create that makes building on Christ's foundation difficult?

2. How secure do you think America is currently in light of verse 2 that "Unless the LORD guards the city [country], the guard keeps watch in vain?"

3. In what ways are children of today an inheritance? If you have children, or are planning for children, what legacy is important to you and your spouse to leave your children?

Psalm of Strength

> "Make me to know your ways,
> O Lord; teach me your paths"
>
> **(Psalm 25:4)**

PSALM OF ASCENT 128

¹ Happy is everyone who fears the Lord,
　　who walks in his ways.
² You shall eat the fruit of the labor of your
　　hands; you shall be happy, and it shall go
　　well with you.
³ Your wife shall be like a fruitful vine
　　within your house,
　　your children will be like olive shoots
　　around your table.
⁴ Thus shall the man be blessed
　　who fears the Lord.
⁵ The Lord bless you from Zion,
　　May you see the prosperity of Jerusalem
　　all the days of your life.
⁶ May you see your children's children.
　　Peace be upon Israel!

REVERENCE FOR THE LORD LEADS TO BLESSINGS

Happy is everyone who fears the LORD.

Psalm 128:1

As families traveled to the holy city for the annual festivals, they mutually rejoiced over how gracious and good God had been to them. They acknowledged that without God in the establishment of their home and lives, life held no meaning. Thus, a home that is built on a godly foundation is a blessed home. Psalm 128 also explores two other areas regarding the habitants of a blessed home: 1) what the hearts of those living in the home looks like in order to receive God's blessings, and 2) the pronouncement of enjoying the after-glow of God's blessings.

Our psalmist, not identified, jumps right into the heart of what it takes to have a happy home. "Happy is everyone who fears the LORD, who walks in his ways" (verse 1). Today, the word **happy** doesn't seem to convey the fullness of the original meaning. Our modern culture has watered down the true meaning of what a blessed life entails. America ties happiness to our circumstances–namely, that if our circumstances are favorable, then we can consider ourselves happy. But this interpretation is incomplete, even shallow. While God does work in our circumstances, and can change them for the better, causing our hearts to be joyful, it is equally untrue that if our circumstances turn unfavorable, we have fallen out of favor with God. This is why I prefer the word **blessed** rather than happy, because I can still feel blessed even though my circumstances have taken a downturn. So, what is involved in being blessed (having the favor of the Lord) rather than simply *feeling* happy?

> **TODAY'S PEARL**
>
> "Let all the earth fear the LORD; let all the inhabitants of the world stand in awe of him" (Psalm 33:8).

There are two meanings to the *fear of the Lord*. However, only one leads to a blessed life.

Fear and Dread of the Unrepentant

This kind of *fear of the Lord* represents terror and dread felt by those who stand proud and unrepentant before God on the Day of Judgment (see Revelation 6:15-17). Isaiah 2:19 says: "Enter the caves of the rocks and the holes of the ground, from the terror of the LORD, and from the glory of his majesty, when he rises to terrify the earth." This verse describes those that will face God's wrath because they have rejected Him. They will scatter in hopes of escaping their doomed fate, but they won't succeed. Eugene Peterson says in his book, *A*

Long Obedience in the Same Direction, "Too many people are willfully refusing to pay attention to the One who wills our happiness and ignorantly supposing that the Christian way is a harder way to get what they want than doing it on their own."[1] A life void of reverence for God and in rebellion to His ways leads to a lifetime of constant vexations and disappointments. God hates pride (Proverbs 16:5), and an unrepentant heart not only cuts a person off from God's blessings, but he won't go unpunished.

Acknowledge, Respect and Wonderment

For those who are in Christ there is no better news then to be declared not guilty. "There is therefore now no condemnation for those who are in Christ Jesus" (Romans 8:1). Believers are in right standing with God because they're united with Christ.[2] For believers *the fear of the Lord* means developing a lifetime attitude of reverence and awe. However, there's more to it than just respect. It is to realize that while God is good, patient, and loving, He is also holy, just, and all-powerful.

> **KEY POINT #1**
>
> He took what was worthless from us (our sin) and gave us what is invaluable (His forgiveness and eternal life) instead

In our prior state, we were on death row, with no hope. We were spiritually dead, enslaved to sin and under God's wrath. But, Jesus made an incredible offer when He died on the cross. For those who accepted His offer of salvation, He made an exchange. We traded our sin for His righteousness. He took what was worthless from us (our sin) and gave us what is invaluable (His forgiveness and eternal life) instead. We went from being under His wrath as children of the dark to His beloved children of the Light. From a life of despair and dread to a life of hopeful anticipation. From the kingdom of Satan to the kingdom of God.

Having a healthy *fear of the Lord* consists of three basic components that leads to blessings and each involves an attitude and an action.

1. An attitude of veneration, or reverence towards the Lord. Our psalmist in verse 1 declares that those who recognize God as Lord, venerates or revers God, will be happy, or blessed. Reverence is a state of profound respect, honor, or awe towards our heavenly Father and ought to include a physical response such as getting down on our knees to bow. Ancient Israel demonstrated their holy regard for God by dropping to their knees. The Hebrew word **Shachah** (shaw-khaw) means to prostrate, as in paying homage to royalty or to God, to bow, or worship.[3] Ephesians 3:14 says: "For this reason I bow my knees before the Father." And Ezra 9:5, "At the evening sacrifice I [Ezra] got up from my fasting, with my garments and my mantle torn, and fell on my knees, spread out my hands to the LORD my God." And Daniel 6:10, "Although Daniel knew that the document had been signed, he continued to go to his house, which had windows in its upper room open toward Jerusalem, and to get down on his knees three times a day to pray to his God and praise him, just as he had done previously." The heart attitude and actions of Daniel and Ezra ought to encourage believers to not only worship the Lord in our hearts and spirits, but also in a physical posture of humility.

> **KEY POINT #2**
>
> Reverence is a state of profound respect, honor, or awe towards our heavenly Father and ought to include a physical response such as getting down on our knees to bow.

In our western society there are two sad realities: (1) a lack of reverence shown towards Jesus for His redeeming sacrifice, and (2) our culture in general robs God of the glory for the personal level of success, affluence, and skills it has attained. Even some believers neglect to give God the honor which is justly due Him. Getting down on our knees or fully prostrated on the floor would keep our egos in check, reminding us that God is the Giver of all we have, including our skills. "A person will only be reverent when he realizes the love of God is upon the obedient but that the wrath of God is upon the disobedient.[4]

2. A Lifestyle of Sweet Obedience. This brings us to the second part of verse 1 "who walks in his ways." A family that is blessed is characterized by having its priorities in the right order, meaning that God is the head of the home. He is highly venerated and given the highest place of honor within its walls. The hearts of the inhabitants prayerfully trust Him with the matters that concern them. He is actively involved in the life of the family, affecting circumstances to bring about His desired will. The family members are cognizant of His participation and can discern His manifestation in the home.

KEY POINT #3

Think of people you have faith in or highly trust. Simply, faith means trusting that God will do what He says He will do. The people we trust are usually the same people we highly respect.

Matthew 8:5-10 tells the story of the Roman soldier whose faith got Jesus' attention. Jesus was in Capernaum when a Roman centurion approached him with a great need.

> "Lord, my servant is lying at home paralyzed, in terrible distress." And he said to him, "I will come and cure him." The centurion answered, "Lord, I am not worthy to have you come under my roof; but only speak the word, and my servant will be healed. For I also am a man under authority, with soldiers under me; and I say to one, 'Go,' and he goes, and to another, 'Come,' and he comes, and to my slave, 'Do this,' and the slave does it." When Jesus heard him, he was amazed and said to those who followed

him, "Truly I tell you, in no one in Israel have I found such faith."

A centurion was a career military officer in the Roman army, in charge of one hundred soldiers.[5] As an officer with authority, the centurion had soldiers under him who highly esteemed him. With authority and respect comes obedience; thus, he knew that out of respect his soldiers would obey when he gave them an order. As such, he could have allowed an attitude towards Jesus of pride, power, money, or even race to become a barrier between him and Jesus.[6] But, none of those things prevented the soldier from approaching Jesus with his request. Why do you think this is?

The Roman centurion acknowledged Jesus' divine position of authority and knew He would do what He claimed He could do–heal his servant. Think of people you have faith in or highly trust. Simply, faith means trusting that God will do what He says He will do. The people we trust are usually the same people we highly respect.

Our desire to be obedient should not be out of fear as if we are under the wrath of God. After all, we are children of the King! When we're in an abiding relationship with Jesus, our obedience and demeanor confirms the Lord's presence living in us. First John 3:24 verifies our position. "All who obey his commandments abide in him, and he abides in them. And by this we know that he abides in us, by the Spirit that he has given us." Choosing to do what pleases the Lord, and giving Him all the glory for the results, produces a blessed life.

3. Fearing the Lord means also hating what is evil. Proverbs 8:13 says: "The fear of the LORD is hatred of evil. Pride and arrogance and the way of evil and perverted speech I hate." The more our love grows for the Lord, the more we reverence Him. "By loyalty and faithfulness iniquity is atoned for, and by the fear of the LORD one avoids evil" (Proverbs 16:6). A genuine desire to live God's way and in obedience to His Word increases our hatred for evil. We will love what God loves and hate what God hates. This also includes the socially accepted sins such as using any means to accomplish our goals or taking advantage of people.[7] God's ways are not only best but they also provide protection. God guards His faithful ones. "The LORD loves those who hate evil; he guards the lives of his faithful; he rescues them from the hand of the wicked" (Psalm 97:10). In our humanness, we have to choose. Choosing to hate means to reject, to love means to choose.[8]

Vines and Olive Shoots

In God's economy, obedience brings blessing, but it's also true that God's blessings have a way of multiplying. "You shall eat the fruit of the labor of your hands; you shall be happy, and it shall go well with you" (verse 2). If what we're doing is what God has proposed for us to do then we'll reap the fruit that comes as a result of our hard work. And if we're doing the work as if we're doing it for the Lord (Colossians 3:23), we'll be at peace with it. The ancient Israelite husband or wife who revered and trusted God profited from their diligent efforts because they went about their God-ordained work with a desire to exalt God through it. By doing so, God blessed this household.

The psalmist begins verses 3 and 4 with references to the godly wife. Because of her diligent and gracious contributions to the home and the warm and hospitable atmosphere she creates, she is described as a fruitful vine. "Your wife will be like a fruitful vine within your house; your children will be like olive shoots around your table" (verse 3). Like a fruitful vine she will be blessed with children, perhaps many children. These children of the home are compared to olive shoots–vines that require support. Much like vines, children are dependent on their parents. Like new shoots from the olive vine, someday their children will marry and have their own seedlings. Herein lies an example of God's blessing of multiplying (or increasing) the family lineage. Thus, there is the mental picture of a home in ancient Israel with several children sitting around a large table like many young, energetic olive shoots full of hope and promise. In verse 4, the psalmist reiterates the answer to what constitutes a blessed life–a godly man, with his wife and children who are sustained by their healthy fear of the Lord and in their keeping to God's ways.

Enjoying the After-Glow of Blessings

Verse 5 reminds me of well-wishes we often say to close military friends or families moving on to their next duty station. "Enjoy the good life in Jerusalem every day of your life" (v. 5 MSG). Today it might sound something like, "We hope you enjoy living in (whatever city it is). We wish you all the best." A good family life isn't automatic. We must pour into it a faith-based life, live according to God's Word, and in the fear of the Lord, trusting that He will meet the needs of our family. From such godly essentials comes the fruit of our hard work. Some of this fruit might be in the form of material blessings, but it is our Lord and Savior in whom we find our true satisfaction. He is the ultimate blessing!

From the context of family comes verse 6–that parents live to see their own olive shoots become parents themselves. "May you see your children's children." God created the family, and out of His immense love for us we respond by living and working in joyful obedience. An attitude of reverence for God + obedience = the ability to enjoy the afterglow of His blessings.

Prayer for a Heart that Reveres the Lord

Lord,

I love Your Word not only because its precepts are true, but they are there to show me and my family how to live in a world that doesn't honor You. Enable my family and me to grow in our reverence and awe of You. Help us to pass a lifestyle of reverence down to our children, so that they will have Your favor, too.

Thank You, Lord for Your sweet blessings upon my family and for the safety You provide. You deserve all the glory and honor for the favor You've shown my family. Cause our hearts to desire to always walk in Your ways and to give you the highest place of honor in our home and in our hearts. Help us to discern the spiritual things You teach us and to trust You for all that concerns us. As we grow in our love for You, make us less and less tolerant of what is hateful, even in the subtlest of ways. And help us to choose things that are pleasing in Your sight.

In the work that we do, let our motivation be to give You the glory so our family will see the fruits of our labor. Amen.

Chapter Nine Key Points

1. He took what was worthless from us (our sin) and gave us what is invaluable (His forgiveness and eternal life) instead.

2. Reverence is a state of profound respect, honor, or awe towards our heavenly Father and ought to include a physical response such as getting down on our knees to bow.

3. Think of people you have faith in or highly trust. Simply, faith means trusting God will do what He says He will do. The people we trust are usually the same people we highly respect.

Reader's Reflections

1. What has been your understanding of the *fear of the Lord*?
2. What is your definition of a *blessed* person? Does it carry the same meaning to you as a *happy* person? Why or why not?
3. If you grew up in a Christian home, what were some of your family's ways of showing reverence, or veneration to our Lord?

Psalm of Strength

"O come, let us worship and bow down,
let us kneel before the LORD, our Maker!"

(Psalm 95:6)

PSALM OF ASCENT 129

[1] "Often have they attacked me from my youth"
      –let Israel now say–
[2] "often have they attacked me from my youth,
      yet they have not prevailed against me.
[3] The plowers plowed on my back;
      they made their furrows long."
[4] The LORD is righteous;
      he has cut the cords of the wicked.
[5] May all who hate Zion
      be put to shame and turned backward.
[6] Let them be like the grass on the housetops
      that withers before it grows up,
[7] with which reapers do not fill their hands
      or binders of sheaves their arms,
[8] while those who pass by do not say,
      "The blessings of the LORD be upon you!
      We bless you in the name of the LORD!"

CHAPTER TEN

GOD LIFTS UP THE DOWNTRODDEN

The LORD is righteous; he has cut the cords of the wicked."
Psalm 129:4

During the course of their nation's history, the Israelites were under constant threat of destruction. The first three verses of this psalm begin with the pilgrims recalling Israel's captivity. Verse 1 describes just how long their tyranny dragged on–"Often have they attacked me from my youth," and their oppression is summed up in two words: ***often and* youth**. The traveling pilgrims reflected on their lengthy history of persecution, remembering their sorrows from their earliest days, and how often they were broken and browbeaten. In all likelihood, many were born into cruel circumstances and never knew ease and autonomy. Perhaps as the pilgrims walked the well-trodden road to Jerusalem, with their heads, arms, and voices lifted up in a posture of praise, they articulated their joy that God never allowed their people to be completely destroyed [1](verse 2). Although weakened from a lifetime of contempt, their enemies never prevailed against them. Therefore the subject of this Song of Ascent is of a heart that trusts God and His sustaining power in times of oppression.

If you're familiar with farming, you'll appreciate the meaning of the agricultural metaphor used in verse 3. "The plowers plowed on my back; they made their furrows long." Our psalmist gives us a profound and troubling imagery. He compares the furrows made in the soil by a plow to the deep oppression the Israelites endured on a regular basis. Fraught with relentless brutal treatment, it was as if their oppressors had plowed deep furrows of intense infliction down their backs. If there is any fresh insight captured in studying the Psalms of Ascent, it is a growing appreciation for the Israelites' endurance as a people. God was again in their corner. From one generation to the next God sustained this nation.

In fact, God's entire Word is about His sustaining might. Some of my family's hardest trials were due to trying and discouraging circumstances that seemed to drag on—a sudden change of homeport in the middle of a school year and my husband, Ray, living as a geographical bachelor for a year and a half. These and other types of obstacles common to the military lifestyle can cripple us in our spirit—causing us to feel as though the military establishment is plowing down our own backs.

Isaiah 61: 1-2 is a crucial passage of Scripture. Besides being a message of the coming Messiah, it alludes to the eventual release of the captives from Babylon and God lifting their oppression.

The spirit of the Lord God is upon me, because the Lord has anointed me; he has sent me to bring good news to the oppressed, to bind up the brokenhearted, to proclaim liberty to the captives, and release to the prisoners; to proclaim the year of the Lord's favor, and the day of vengeance of our God; to comfort all who mourn; to provide for those who mourn; to provide for those who mourn in Zion–to give them a garland instead of ashes, the oil of gladness instead of mourning, the mantle of praise instead of a faint spirit.

Because of their disobedience and rebellion to God, the ancient pilgrims became captives of Babylon. They knew no peace and their lives were void of God's blessing. But now, God was about to do a **new thing** for His people (Isaiah 43:19). As the great Guardian of the Israelites, He used King Cyrus of Persia to set a large group of captives free.

Justice for Israel

In Psalm 124 we touched on the subject of God as Defender. We revisit Him as Israel's Defender again briefly in Psalm 129:4. "The Lord is righteous; he has cut the cords of the wicked." Here "the wicked" is referring to those against a faith in the one true God. The time of reckoning had finally come. God rises to vindicate Israel, ending their captivity from the Babylonians. No more will they dig furrows of tyranny on the backs of Israel. Isaiah 51:22-23 gives God's promise to redeem Israel.

> **KEY POINT #1**
>
> God will never abandon you. He promises to be your Deliverer when you face oppression of any kind. (Psalm 9:9).

Thus says your Sovereign, the LORD, your God who pleads the cause of his people: See, I have taken from your hand the cup of staggering; [Israel's sin] you shall drink no more from the bowl of my wrath. And I will put it into the hand of your tormentors, who have said to you, "Bow down, that we may walk on you"; and you have made your back like the ground and like the street for them to walk on.

In reading the above Scripture passage, you may have made a vivid connection between Israel's tormentors plowing down their backs and the scourging to our despised and rejected Savior's back (John 19:1). Like Israel, Jesus was familiar with heartache and sorrow. His death not only achieved redemption–freedom and liberation from the bondage of sin and death for all believers–but prior to Jesus' arrival, God provided a different kind of freedom, a physical release from a life of captivity. Isaiah prophesied that God's chosen servant, Jesus, would bring justice for the oppressed. "He will not grow faint or be crushed until he has established justice in the earth" (Isaiah 42:4).

If you've reached a place in which the challenges of the military life have you in an oppressive existence and you struggle to remain steadfast and wholly committed, God promises to be your source of strength. "Seek the Lord and his strength; seek His presence continually" (Psalm 105:4). If we daily seek Him for healing of a downtrodden spirit, He'll cut the cords of oppression. But it takes a patient heart and a committed faith. By trusting in God's Word, He'll produce a harvest even from the channels carved out from oppression. And in due time, He will draw you out from the pit of gloom and "set my [your] feet upon a rock, making my [your] steps secure" (Psalm 40:2). The righteous, who remain close to God, will be lifted up and supplied with enough strength to stay the course. God will never abandon you. He promises to be your Deliverer when you face oppression of any kind. (Psalm

9:9). When the demands of the military life have you down, look to Jesus to encourage and lift your heart and head.

A word of concern here: If you think you are experiencing symptoms of depression, I strongly recommend reaching out

KEY POINT #2

Part of God's redeeming power is to give us freedom to live fully in Him. It is difficult to do that if we're under bondage or oppression to something or someone.

to your physician. With the right medical treatment combined with a strong faith in our great Healer, life can be better managed. Indeed, faith makes a difference when struggling with adverse circumstances. Psalm 3:3 says: "But you, O Lord, are a shield around me, my glory, and the one who lifts my head." Part of God's redeeming power is to give us freedom to live fully in Him. It is difficult to do that if we're under bondage or oppression to something or someone.

As you may have noticed, there is a shift in the middle of this psalm from remembering the plight of the oppressed to Israel's persecutors. At first glance, verse 5 appears unforgiving, even vindictive. "May all who hate Zion be put to shame and turned backward." Is our psalmist asking God to bring evil upon the lives of their oppressors? In order to answer that question, we must first understand a key truth about God. Since He reigns overall, His plans for His children are certain; nothing and no one can spoil them. God's protection of the faithful means that His justice can include foiling the schemes of those who would harm them.[3] This prayer is called an imprecation or a curse on Jerusalem's enemies.[4] It called for God to bring humiliation upon those who hated Jerusalem because they schemed evil. The psalmist likened their wicked schemes to the frivolous nature of blades of grass growing on housetops (v. 6). After a spring rain, tiny blades of grass sprouted on the roof tops of homes. In the heat of the summer day, these blades of grass void of adequate soil, would succumb to the heat.

The curse portrayed here is that Jerusalem's enemies would also fade away as quickly as grass atop rooftops. Even reapers have no interest in harvesting this grass as it is insignificant and holds no useful purpose (verse 7).

For twenty-first century believers this imprecatory psalm doesn't give us permission to pronounce curses on our enemies. Scripture such as Proverbs 24:17-18 teaches: "Do not rejoice when your enemies fall and do not let your heart be glad when they stumble, or else the Lord will see it and be displeased, and turn away his anger from them." We are encouraged not to rejoice at the misfortunes of others, even if we think they deserve them.[5] Instead, we take our cues from Jesus. "But I say to you, Love your enemies, and pray for those who persecute you" (Matthew 5:44). We can begin loving our enemies by simply praying for them. Natural selfishness can make praying for our enemies difficult. If this is the case, and we've fully given ourselves to the Lord, we can ask Him to show us how to do this. Jesus taught this, but He also lived it. He died on the cross for all, even for His enemies.

When we know that evil people are seeking to harm our country, we can ask God to fight on our behalf. The ancient Israelites prayed that the schemes of their pursuers would fail, and that the pursuers themselves would suffer disappointment, humiliation, and finally destruction.[6] A Christian nation must protect itself from those who seek to do evil, but in addition to military engagement, we're to also pray for God's justice. In his prayers, King David left room for God to avenge him. "Contend, O LORD, with those who contend with me; fight against those who fight against me!" God's justice is far more thorough than ours ever could be.

Like the ancient Israelites, America has enemies. The terrorists who carried out the September 11, 2001, attacks have indeed plowed a furrow down the backs of Americans with their evil act. Although foreign terrorists haven't physically oppressed the United States for centuries in the same manner Israel's enemies did, nonetheless their evil agenda burdens our minds. Even the word *terrorism* exemplifies oppressive thinking. Isaiah 59:6-8 is quite possibly a vivid portrayal of terrorists today:

> Their works are works of iniquity, and deeds of violence are in their hands. Their feet run to evil, and they rush to shed innocent blood; their thoughts are thoughts of iniquity, desolation and destruction are in their highways. The way of peace they do not know, and there is no justice in their paths. Their roads they have made crooked; no one who walks in them knows peace.

I'll be honest: Jesus' words to love my enemies feels unnatural. However, as believers, we're called to look at Jesus' commands regarding our enemies through the lens of His love and His example. Second Peter 3:9 tells us that "the Lord is…not wanting *any* to perish, but all to come to repentance." The same grace He gave you and me, He also extends to our enemies. There is no one that God isn't able to save and bring into a relationship with His Son, Jesus. Our prayers may not stop global terrorism, but God can use our prayers to reach those individuals who are searching for the one who is Truth, which fits the bill for *any* in 2 Peter 3:9.

Regarding the ever-growing threat of terrorism, Americans must stand with our military because the threat is here to stay. This burden isn't just our

KEY POINT #3

We cannot allow ourselves to think America can't be breached; we must reject apathy and stand against sin and evil. We need to pray that our enemies will not prevail against us, but that they become insignificant as withered grass, having no opportunity to germinate and spread their evil.

military's battle, but a war for all Americans. We can't be passive onlookers. We must be attentive to the world of terrorism and pray regularly that evil schemes come to light and are foiled. We must pray for God to protect innocent people and ask Him to intervene with His mighty hand. It isn't just a physical battle, but a spiritual one as well. Satan's goal is to lead as many as possible astray down the crooked road of evil. He doesn't give up and neither should we. Terrorists' tactics and their hidden schemes exposes their work as Satan's.

We cannot allow ourselves to think America can't be breached; we must reject apathy and stand against sin and evil. We need to pray strategically that our enemies will not prevail against us, but that they become as insignificant as withered grass, having no opportunity to germinate and spread their evil. This is why verse 8 of Psalm 129 says that the oppressors with wicked agendas will not receive the praise of passersby's. "While those who pass by do not say, 'The blessing of the LORD be upon you!'" The Bible makes one thing clear–war is inevitable. However, God promises in His Word that He has the final victory. He will turn intimidators and oppressors backward (verse 5). He will cut off their evil cords and bring shame down upon their heads.

Prayer for God to Sustain America
Lord,

Your Word says in Psalm 9:9-10 that You are a "stronghold for the oppressed, a stronghold in times of trouble." No matter what the oppression is, You promise to be with me and are the lifter of my head. I pray for Your peace because it surpasses all understanding (Philippians 4:6-8). Help me not to succumb to defeat in my spirit, but claim victory in Christ.

Lord, terrorism abounds today. Make me more attentive to what is going on around the globe so my prayers will be effective (James

5:16). Don't let me become apathetic in praying over our nation and our military for protection from our enemies. Instead, call me out to be a watchman like the sentinels of long ago who stood on the walls to their cities watching and listening for signs of the enemy. "Deliver me [Americans], O LORD, protect [all Americans everywhere] from evildoers; protect [us] from those who are violent, who plan evil things in their minds and stir up wars continually. The arrogant have hidden a trap for [us], and with cords they have spread a net, along the road they have set snares for me [us]" (Psalm 140:1-2, 5).

Lord, give our service members vigilance in battle with the enemy. Psalm 144:1 says: "Blessed be the LORD, my rock, who trains my hands for war, and my fingers for battle." And, "Let all those be put to shame who seek to snatch away [our lives]; let those be turned back and brought to dishonor who desire [our country's]hurt" (Psalm 40:14). Today there are countries in the midst of civil wars, and nations—some good, others bad, crumbling—ripe for terrorism to gain a foothold. Bring to light and spoil all plans of evil. Cut the evil cords they sow and bring justice upon their heads. Cause America's enemies to become as insignificant as blades of withered grass, unable to spread their evil. I pray for a hedge of protection along America's borders and around those on the frontlines of battle. Amen.

Chapter Ten Key Points

1. God will not step on you then abandon you. He promises to be your vindicator when you face oppression of any kind. (Psalm 9:9).

2. Part of God's redeeming power is to give us freedom to live fully in Him. It is difficult to do that if we're under bondage or oppression to something or someone.

3. We cannot allow ourselves to think America can't be breached. We must reject apathy and stand against sin and evil. We

need to pray that our enemies will not prevail against us, but that they become insignificant as withered grass, having no opportunity to germinate and spread their evil.

Reader's Reflections

1. Have you experienced a season of oppression? If so, how did prayer and your faith factor into your circumstances?
2. How has God used that experience to minister to others?
3. What is your perception of the wicked today? Does it seem like they're flourishing, going unpunished? Why or why not?

Psalm of Strength

"He heals the brokenhearted, and binds up their wounds"
(Psalm 147:3).

PSALM OF ASCENT 130

¹ Out of the depths I cry to you, O Lord.
² Lord, hear my voice!
    Let your ears be attentive
    to the voice of my supplications!
³ If you, O Lord, should mark iniquities,
    Lord, who could stand?
⁴ But there is forgiveness with you,
    so that you may be revered.
⁵ I wait for the Lord, my soul waits,
    and in his word I hope;
⁶ my soul waits for the Lord
    more than those who watch for the morning,
    more than those who watch for the morning.
⁷ O Israel, hope in the Lord!
    For with the Lord there is steadfast love,
    and with him is great power to redeem.
⁸ It is he who will redeem Israel
    from all its iniquities.

A MERCIFUL GOD

"My soul waits for the LORD more than those who watch for
the morning, more than those who watch for the morning."
Psalm 130:6

In the previous Psalm of Ascent, we saw how the Israelite's ongoing oppression by their enemies was like a plow digging furrows down their backs. But God extended His mercy and justice and lifted their downtrodden spirits by breaking their cords of oppression. In Psalm 130 the psalmist's focus is on a different kind of oppression. This time, perhaps the furrow plowed down his back is that of his own sin.[1] The psalmist is in a state of remorse and deep distress, cries out to God. From the far reaches of his soul, he pleads for God to turn His ears towards him and listen to his urgent prayer.

Out of the depths, I cry to you, O Lord. Lord, hear my voice! Let your ears be attentive to the voice of my supplications! (vv.1-2).

Despair can do two things: It can drive us farther away from God–isolation, or draw us closer to Him–inclusion. When it causes us to fall away from God, despair can send us into the fox hole of feeling sorry for ourselves which only deepens our hopelessness. If, instead, we follow our psalmist's example and cry out to God, our heart's focus turns to the only One who can help.[2] Even in times of wretched aloneness, we are assured we are never missing from His presence. For our psalmist, his sin is the catalyst that draws him to call on God.

There are many reasons believers come to a faith in Jesus and each one has a testimony. No two are exactly alike. However, all believers have one thing in common–sin.

Sin is the wall *we* erect between us and God. It leads to death. If you grew up attending Sunday school, it is likely you learned Romans 6:23: "For the wages of sin is death, but the free gift of God is eternal life in Christ Jesus our Lord." Sin prohibits us from living close with God as sin and a holy God cannot co-exist. Thus we must choose between two ways we want to be paid in this life–with sin's currency, which is death and complete isolation from God, or Christ's currency, which is perpetual life in God's presence.[3] And the deal gets better–it's completely free.

In the book of Micah, the prophet cautioned the people of Judah about God's looming judgment, forewarning them about Babylon's coming destruction of Jerusalem because of the people's sin and their indifference to God's purposes. They blended in with the culture, becoming indistinguishable. By this

---

TODAY'S PEARL

"For you, O Lord are good and forgiving, abounding in steadfast love to all who call on you" (Psalm 86:5).

time, the situation had grown severe enough that God no longer extended His favor. "But they kept mocking the messengers of God, despising his words, and scoffing at his prophets, until the wrath of the LORD against his people became so great that there was no remedy" (2 Chronicles 36:16). Herein lays a warning to us as well. Our culture takes the habit of sin too lightly. However, it is no small matter. God takes sin seriously and because He does, so should we. As God has promised in His Word, there will come a day when He'll remove His hand of mercy and spread out His hand of judgment instead.[4] Conversely, Micah also reveals God's compassionate nature.

> Where is another God like you, who pardons the sins of the survivors among his people? You cannot stay angry with your people forever, because you delight in showing mercy. Once again you will have compassion on us. You will trample our sins under your feet and throw them into the depths of the ocean (Micah 7:18-19 NLT).

In fact, God offered many opportunities for His children to repent and return to true obedience and worship before judgment arrived.[5] It is reasonable for us to accept that God not only can and does forgive our sins, but in doing so, He also forgives completely, holding no resentment. We attribute this truth to the simple fact that He is God. When we confess our sins, He harbors nothing against us. It is much harder for us to forgive ourselves or to forgive others in the

---

KEY POINT #1

Our psalmist captured, with appreciation, the vastness of our Lord's compassion and grace, that without such grace, no one could stand.

---

same complete way God does, a point that only magnifies certain unknowable aspects of God's holy nature.

The other side of this equation is to consider the alternative consequence in verse 3. "If you, O LORD, should mark iniquities [keep a record], Lord, who could stand?" Amazed at the insight of our psalmist, he captured, with appreciation, the vastness of our Lord's compassion and grace that without such grace no one can stand. God, who desires to pardon our sins, willingly does so when we ask. "But there is forgiveness with you, so that you may be revered" (v. 4). The psalmist draws our attention to what the proper response to such an incredible gift ought to be. Because God loves deeply and freely forgives, He withholds punishment that is genuinely justified. This truth alone should move our hearts to worship and give honor to Him.

King David also penned a similar question. "Who shall ascend the hill of the LORD? And who shall stand in his holy place?"(Psalm 24:3). David promptly answers, "Those who have clean hands and pure hearts, who do not lift up their souls to what is false, and do not swear deceitfully [telling lies under oath]" (v.4). Only those who have "confessed with [their] lips that Jesus is Lord and believe in [their] heart that God raised him from the dead, will be saved" (Romans 10:9). Those who have clean hands. "Wash me thoroughly from my iniquity, and cleanse me from my sin" (Psalm 51:2). Those who have pure hearts. "Lord, who could stand?" (Psalm 130:3). Those who have been reconciled with God. "Therefore, since we are justified by faith, we have peace with God through our Lord Jesus Christ, through whom we have obtained access to this grace in which we stand" (Romans 5:1-2). As believers, we have been declared not guilty (justified) in God's sight; we'll be able to stand with Jesus one day.

The Night Watchmen

> I wait for the LORD, my soul waits, and in his word I hope;
> my soul waits for the LORD more than those who watch for
> the morning, more than those who watch for the morning
> (vv. 5-6).

Did you catch the heightened sense of longing with the repeating of verse 6? I find myself drawn to this metaphor. As a Navy wife, duty days or duty weekends were often an interruption in the life and rhythm of our military family. I sometimes dreaded them as they approached, while at the same time longed to get them over with. Duty days and weekends served a necessary objective, however, and I fully understood their vital purpose–a purpose that was used in Bible times, and a tradition that lives on today in the ranks of our military.

You may be familiar with the high walls that surrounded ancient cities. They suggest a sense of safety and community. Their purpose was to protect those living within its walls. The night watchmen, akin to our modern-day servicemen and women fulfilling their *duty watch*, had an important role–one they took seriously.

While the city peacefully slept, the citizens trusted the night watchmen to defend them. Night after night the watchmen stood on the wall watching for any approaching threat. They defended the wall at all costs in hopes of preventing the enemy from breaching and overtaking it. There would be no falling asleep on the night watch. Just one slip could prove fatal for the sleeping city. On those quiet and uneventful nights, in which time slowed down to a crawl, dawn couldn't come soon enough. But the opposite was true as well. If the night watchmen caught a dim glimpse of foes scrimmaging in the black of night, a horrendous battle ensued. For these night watchmen, they longed for the night of dreadful fighting to end, and for the sun to spill over the eastern horizon.

Sweet Redemption

Our psalmist likens the watchmen watching for the dawn of a new morning to his personal longing for God to extend His mercy and wipe out all the wrong he did. But the urgency of his heart is so desperate that his soul waits and hopes for God's mercy and forgiveness *even more than those who watch for the morning,* more than those sitting on the wall anxious for the sun to rise. The culmination of his sin has risen to the forefront of his heart and propelled him to place all of his hopes in the God who created the gift of forgiveness and salvation.

> O Israel, hope in the LORD! For with the Lord there is steadfast love, and with him is great power to redeem. It is he who will redeem Israel from all its iniquities (vv. 7-8).

The psalmist extended his bidding to his people and pleaded for them to humble themselves before God, and call upon Him while there was still time for the forgiveness of sin. There should be no fear. If God loved them with a steadfast love in all their rebellion, He would still love them with a repentant heart. Yes, God redeemed Israel, but also

---

KEY POINT #2

If God loved them with a steadfast love in all their rebellion, He would still love them with a repentant heart

---

redeems the one today who fears there isn't enough redemption to blot out his terrible sins. Christ died for all. His forgiveness excludes no one.[6] Without Christ's atonement for sin there would be nothing to look forward to. Whatever moments of fleeting happiness we'd experience in this life would be spoiled by the dread of coming punishment. But because of God's loving plan, we are people of hope and light. Our hearts are brimming with joy over the promise of Christ's presence.

Like the people of Micah's era, there is evidence today that believers are blending into our modern culture, becoming less recognizable as God's children. Sadly, there are also believers that are indifferent to God's plans and purposes. Is it possible that the light of Christ in the hearts of God's children is dimming in our dark world? Ephesians 5:6 is our encouragement to keep our light strong. "For once you were darkness, but now in the Lord you are light. Live as children of light." Our lives should reflect behavior that authenticates Jesus' presence in us and validates our faith.[7]

Whenever I read Psalm 130 I'm humbled. If our Lord kept a record of all of our sinful indulgences, misdeeds, wrongs, iniquities and immoralities, truly, who could stand? It is in this stark contrast that I contemplate the magnitude of His love that motivates the sweet redemption He graciously offers.

Prayer for the Forgiveness of Sin

Lord,

Thank You for the gift of confession. I am grateful that You created confession because You *desire* to forgive us. You went so far as to allow Your Son to die just so You could exonerate my sin. First John 1:9 is Your promise and my assurance that You forgive completely. "As far as the east is from the west, so far he removes our transgressions from us" (Psalm 103:12). I know that my sin creates a wall between us. Therefore, because I desire closeness with You, I repent and ask for Your forgiveness of my sin(s)for:_____. I realize I don't deserve forgiveness because of my transgressions, "but with You there is forgiveness" (Psalm 130:4). You don't keep a record of all my wrongs. Because of Your steadfast love and Your abundant redemption" (Psalm 130:7) Your grace redeems my life. Thank You, Lord, that when I confess, You forgive and forget. You wipe my slate clean. I am as far away from my sin as east is from the west. Draw me close to You and to Your Word so that I can be strengthened by Your Spirit to avoid sin's temptation.

Lord, show me how to extend forgiveness to others when they have wronged me. Put forgiveness in my heart. Don't let an attitude of bitterness or resentment take hold, but help me to forgive in full like You do. Show me ways to reach out to others who are snared by sin. Instead of judging them, give me the right words to convey that You desire to also forgive them.

If my heart has become indifferent to Your purposes and I have blended in with my culture, awaken my heart, Lord, and put an urgency in it like our psalmist whose "soul waits for the LORD, and in his word I hope; more than those who watch for the morning" (Psalm 130:5). Hide Your Word in my heart so I will desire to continually seek Your forgiveness and Your purpose for my life. Let Your sweet redemption always be a reminder of Your abundant mercy, for there is no other god that offers forgiveness and restores me to right standing before You. Amen.

Chapter Eleven Key Points

1. Our psalmist captured, with appreciation the enormity of our Lord's compassion and grace, that without such grace no one can stand. God, who desires to pardon our sins, willingly does so when we ask.

2. If God loved them with a steadfast love in all their rebellion, He would still love them with a repentant heart.

Reader's Reflections

1. In what types of situations has your heart led you to call out to God?

2. In your estimation, are believers today allowing the light of Christ's presence in their lives to dim? Why or why not? If so, what evidence do you see in the world to support your view?

3. Would you agree with the statement that "it is harder for most of us to either forgive ourselves or to forgive others in the same complete way God does, without residual resentment?"

4. When you consider your sin, is there remorse that prompts urgency in your heart to bring it before the Lord, like our psalmist did?

Psalm of Strength

"Happy are those whose transgression
is forgiven, whose sin is covered"
(Psalm 32:1).

PSALM OF ASCENT 131

¹ O Lord, my heart is not lifted up,
  my eyes are not raised too high;
  I do not occupy myself with things
  too great and too marvelous
  for me.
² But I have calmed and quieted my soul,
  like a weaned child with its mother;
  my soul is like the weaned child that is
  with me.
³ O Israel, hope in the Lord
  from this time on and forevermore.

HUMILITY LEADS TO CONTENTMENT

"O LORD, my heart is not lifted up,
my eyes are not raised too high."
Psalm 131:1

Jonathan Edwards said this about humility:

A truly humble man is sensible of his natural distance from God; of his dependence on Him; of the insufficiency of his own power and wisdom; and that it is by God's power that he is upheld and provided for, and that he needs God's wisdom to lead and guide him, and His might to enable him to do what he ought to do for Him.[1]

This Psalm of Ascent is a portrait of humility. Again, written by David, who strived to demonstrate humility, struggled at times to maintain a balance between self-loathing and pride. This psalm with its theme of

KEY POINT #1

Humility is closely associated with reverencing the Lord. When we fear the Lord, we acknowledge He is eternal in holiness and in His majesty.

seeking the fruit of humility was the ideal psalm to sing by our traveling pilgrims. It created the right heart attitude before entering the temple. Its single metaphor describes a soul that is calm and content because of a quiet and humble trust in the Lord for all of life's unknowables.

In chapter nine we read that to fear the Lord is to view God with an attitude of reverence and awe. Humility is closely associated with reverencing the Lord. When we fear the Lord, we acknowledge He is eternal in holiness and in His majesty. We recognize He is the Giver of what sustains us–the wisdom and discernment that directs our steps, the provision He provides, His protection over our lives, and the gifts and abilities He has equipped us with. Because He is such, God alone deserves all the praise and credit. Furthermore, we are dependent on God for the outcome of all our undertakings.

Our psalmist models for us an excellent way to praise God. "O LORD, my heart is not lifted up, my eyes are not raised too high"(v.1). Because our psalmist knows the Lord looks intently on the heart, he begins there. Having the right heart attitude is quintessential if we want God to respond to our prayers.

The word humble is the opposite of the word pride. It means having a modest opinion of one's value or importance. Having one's heart inflated and

KEY POINT #2

By yielding to others, we are honoring Christ.

eyes raised are expressions of arrogance and pride. Therefore, pride is an overestimation of our own value and importance.

First Peter 5:5 says, "And all of you must clothe yourselves with humility in your dealings with one another." In today's society there's a growing indifference between young people and the older generation. Pride can become an obstacle for the young to listen and acquire wisdom and knowledge from their elders and the older generation from trying to understand young people.[2] Peter urges both groups to show humility by admitting that they can learn from each other.[3]

Submitting to others also encompasses a teachable spirit. Indeed, we are people who are overly concerned with our station in life and we desire gratitude and approval for the work we do. First Peter 5:6 says "Humble yourselves therefore under the mighty hand of God, so that he may exalt you in due time." Peter reminds us that God will exalt His children at the proper time–either in this life or in our eternal home. God sees what we do now and having His recognition should be our focus rather than overly striving for man's approval. God isn't against our desire to advance in rank or attain that next promotion, but what He does oppose is a person whose heart's chief goal is merely to attain power and wealth. Exclusively seeking wealth and prestige can askew our spiritual vision, leading us to place our security in money and possessions rather than in God.

Does submitting to others mean we must always give into their preferences? No. It means to yield to instruction as well as correction by others. It means setting aside our pride in order to be willing to grow in skill, knowledge, or wisdom by yielding to others and receiving what they have to offer us for our ultimate good. By doing this, we are honoring Christ. "For though the LORD is high, he regards the lowly; but the haughty he perceives from far away" (Psalm 138:6). This verse carries both a benefit and a consequence. When God sees a humble heart He draws close. His presence is with us and He hears our prayers. However, when He identifies a prideful heart, He distances Himself. If a believer refuses to repent or is in a state of rebellion, God won't hear his prayers. "If I had cherished iniquity in my heart, the LORD would not have listened" (Psalm 66:18). This isn't to mean that we have to recall and repent every single sin, but it refers to a reverential habit of confession and obedience.[4]

> **KEY POINT #3**
>
> Pride overestimates our own value and importance, ignoring God's role in our lives and all our endeavors, including our successes and achievements... Pride refers to those who resist God's authority and leadership and believe they can manage without the benefit of God's assistance.

Today, pride is interpreted from a different understanding. The world has stripped the sinful nature of the word and elevated its position, making it less offending. But God's Word doesn't view pride in the same manner as the world views it. There's a difference between being proud of certain things or people–such as I'm proud of my children, or I'm proud of my country–and being prideful. The sin of being prideful overestimates our own value and importance, ignoring God's role in our lives and endeavors, including our successes and achievements. In Scripture, God calls this type of pride sin. "For if those who are nothing think they are something, they deceive themselves" (Galatians 6:3). To God, pride is a serious offense, going back to the Garden of Eden. It is one of the seven sins God deems deadly and despises (Proverbs 6:16-19). Pride refers to those who resist God's authority and leadership and believe they can manage without the benefit of God's assistance. We read in chapter nine that when we walk in God's ways and live in obedience to His Word, we will grow to love what He loves and hate what He hates. God's Word blatantly says in Proverbs 8:13 that "pride and arrogance and the way of evil and perverted speech I hate." If God feels this way, so should we.

Unlike humility, a person with a proud heart isn't teachable because he believes his abilities are superior to others. If we perceive our abilities in this light, it will lead to commending ourselves rather than giving the glory to God. He doesn't object to self-confidence, a healthy self-esteem, or feeling good about an accomplishment, but what He does object to is our foolish attitude of taking full credit for what He has done, or for having an attitude of superiority over others.[5]

King Hezekiah had been an honorable king, but just after his brush with death (2 Kings 20:1-11) in which God healed him and gave him fifteen additional years of life, he became prideful. When Babylon envoys came to see for themselves Hezekiah's miraculous healing, his pride surfaced, revealing the true condition of his heart. "Hezekiah welcomed them; he showed them all his treasure house, the silver, the gold, the spices, the precious oil, his armory, all that was found in his storehouses; there was nothing in his house or in all his realm that Hezekiah did not show them" (2 Kings 20:13).

TODAY'S PEARL

"Humble yourselves therefore under the mighty hand of God, so that he may exalt you in due time" (1 Peter 5:6).

Hezekiah congratulated himself before his guests, taking full credit for his accomplishments and for all his treasures he had accumulated.[6] God had given Hezekiah blessings of success, wealth, honor, and favor, but Hezekiah wrongly used them to impress his guests.[7] When God has stepped into our circumstances and blessed us, we become foolish if we use it to glorify or esteem ourselves. How ironic that there would be a day in which all of Hezekiah's wealth would be carried off by the same Babylonians when the Israelites became their captives.

No Concern for Matters Too Great

The second half of verse 1 refers to matters that are too great for us to be overly concerned about. "I do not occupy myself with things too great and too marvelous for me" (v. 1). This verse is spoken in a spirit of humility and shouts trust and contentment. As the spouse of a chief petty officer, there were situations that came up over the span of my husband's military career that I didn't understand about the military. From my vantage point it didn't make sense, and from the military's perspective, it wasn't necessary for them to explain it to me. Likewise, God has not made us privy to everything He knows. Deuteronomy 29:29 says, "The secret things belong to the LORD our God, but the revealed things belong to us and to our children forever, to observe all the words of this law." God didn't make us with the capacity to understand all aspects of Himself or in the universe. There are things God has chosen to keep top-secret, known only to Him. God is infinite and all-knowing; He didn't give us the capacity to know everything He does.[8]

The good news is that God has revealed to us what He deems necessary in order for us to know enough. Because of His Word we know enough about Him to be saved by faith.[9]

In the military lifestyle there are perplexing circumstances which will test your level of contentment. You may sense a nagging dissatisfaction with your life. If there is discontentment settling in your soul over your circumstances, you may look at the lives of others and secretly covet their togetherness. If you have civilian friends, you wonder how your life would be if you and your family were also civilian. You may even ask yourself, *Would I be happier, more satisfied, more content?* Once we find one culprit to pin our discontentment on, we'll find others. The apostle Paul said in Philippians 4:11, "Not that I am referring to being in need; for I have learned to be content with whatever I have." Notice that this verse is in the present tense. It isn't referring to some other time in the past or in the future, but right now.

Until God changes our current situation, we are to work at being content in the here and now. In our humanity, we may think seeking worldly pursuits will fill our longing to be content, but they are counterfeit. True and lasting contentment is found only in one person–Jesus. Isaiah 55:1-2 addresses the subject of discontentment.

> "Ho, everyone who thirsts, come to the waters; and you that have no money, come, buy and eat! Come, buy wine and milk without money and without price. Why do you spend your money for that which is not bread, and your labor for that which does not satisfy? Listen carefully to me, and eat what is good, and delight yourselves in rich food."

How do we get rid of the vague sense of discontentment we sometimes feel? We must learn the habit of leaning on Christ's power and sufficiency. Paul was content because he learned to focus on the task at hand.[9] He also disconnected himself from nonessentials in order to concentrate on the eternal. If you are the spouse of a military member, your contentment might include a similar action. You may have to prune some nonessentials from your life or add essentials into it. For example, if you're in the midst of a deployment, or your spouse is away at school or undergoing training exercises, consider joining a Christian military spouse support group, a Bible study, or an organization geared to meeting the needs of military and their spouses. Civilian friends are also a wonderful support system, but keep in mind they may not be able to fully appreciate the complexities, the demands, or the range of emotions unique to the military lifestyle. My family became very close to two civilian families during my husband's time on active duty. Because both of our extended families lived in different parts of the country, these two families were an immense blessing and are now a piece of the fabric that makes up part of my overall experience as a military wife.

I've also had the experience of a few civilians who made insensitive comments (not realizing it, of course) about the military lifestyle that caused my contentment to unravel a bit. Ray had just left on deployment and my emotions were tender and raw. For a time, I had to limit my exposure with them until the fabric of this military wife became more durable.

For the issues that are out of our control or for matters we're not permitted to know, we can't let them occupy our hearts and minds to the point it causes us restlessness. If we don't lay out before the Lord, our restless state of being and the ways of the military we don't like or understand, those matters will fester until restlessness hijacks our contentment. We are called to put on humility. Humility declares that God knows what's best. Humility acknowledges God is in control. If we've allowed God to lead our lives, it means we must leave matters beyond our understanding to Him. It is in this frame of reference that our humility will keep us content.

Lastly, there's an element of mystery here in David's words "too great and too marvelous for me" (v.1). God can do marvelous things. The Bible is full of amazing feats God executed. The mystery is that we can't grasp such marvels. David compares his contentment to that of a weaned child whose soul is calm and quiet because his inner battle is over. The child successfully detaches from his mother and is now at rest, trusting his nourishment will come by another method. When we, too, stop demanding to have our pride scratched and adopt a quiet trust in God, we will find contentment for our souls, whether the issues are too immense, difficult, or marvelous.

Prayer for a Contented Heart

Lord,

No one can fathom Your greatness. You choose to reach down to earth and touch our hearts, minds, and lives–from the wellspring of Your love. I humble myself in Your presence and declare You worthy of all my praise.

Thank You, Father, for sending Jesus, our finest example of humility. Show me how to be "gentle and humble in heart" (Matthew 11:29).

I confess those times when pride settled in my heart. I ask for Your forgiveness. I don't want my sin to build a wall between us. Encourage my heart to continually seek You and protect my heart from wandering from Your Word, because it satisfies my soul and ruts out discontentment.

Lord, I recognize that You are the Provider of all I have. You are the strength that sustains me. I may have skill and knowledge, but You gave me those abilities to witness and to serve You. I may be a person of high rank, but You put me in that role to lead others responsibly and to serve out Your purposes in the spirit of humility. Teach me how to yield to others so I can honor Christ. And when corrected by another believer, shield my heart from harboring resentment. Develop humility in me so I can admit when I am wrong. I pray for the discernment to see myself as You do.

In times of discontentment, especially with matters too great and complex for me to comprehend, whether they are militarily related or not, let my humility develop trust and contentment in You, because its benefit is a peaceful spirit. When restless or agitated, direct my heart back to You, reminding me that You know everything there is to know and what is best for me and my family. I acknowledge that You are in control. Show me ways to develop contentment in my present situation, until such time You change my circumstances. May any discontentment I feel drive me to You. Amen.

Chapter Twelve Key Points

1. Humility is closely associated with reverencing the Lord. When we fear the Lord, we acknowledge God is eternal in holiness and in His majesty.
2. By yielding to others we are honoring Christ.
3. Pride overestimates our own value and importance, ignoring God's role in our lives and in all our endeavors, including our successes and achievements. Pride refers to those who resist God's authority and leadership and believe they can get by without God's help.

Reader's Reflections

1. How do you regard humility in a person's character?
2. Does the second half of verse 1 indicate a license to ignore issues?
3. Describe ways pride can affect matters that are beyond our understanding.

Psalm of Strength

"O God, you are my God, I seek you, my soul thirsts for you; my flesh faints for you, as in a dry and weary land where there is no water. So I have looked upon you in the sanctuary, beholding your power and glory"

(Psalm 63:1-2).

PSALM OF ASCENT 132

¹ O LORD, remember in David's favor
 all the hardships he endured;
² how he swore to the LORD
 and vowed to the Mighty One of Jacob,
³ "I will not enter my house
 or get into my bed;
⁴ I will not give sleep to my eyes
 or slumber to my eyelids,
⁵ until I find a place for the LORD,
 a dwelling place for the Mighty One of Jacob."
⁶ We heard of it in Ephrathah;
 we found it in the fields of Jaar.
⁷ "Let us go to his dwelling place;
 let us worship at his footstool."
⁸ Rise up, O LORD, and go to your resting place,
 you and the ark of your might.
⁹ Let your priests be clothed with righteousness,
 and let your faithful shout for joy.
¹⁰ For your servant David's sake
 do not turn away the face of your
 anointed one.

^{11} The LORD swore to David a sure oath
     from which he will not turn back:
     "One of the sons of your body
     I will set on your throne.
^{12} If your sons keep my covenant
     and my decrees that I shall teach them,
     their sons also, forevermore,
     shall sit on your throne."
^{13} For the LORD has chosen Zion;
     he has desired it for his habitation:
^{14} "This is my resting place forever;
     here I will reside, for I have desired it.
^{15} I will abundantly bless its provisions;
     I will satisfy its poor with bread.
^{16} Its priests I will clothe with salvation,
     and its faithful will shout for joy.
^{17} There I will cause a horn to sprout up
     for David;
     I have prepared a lamp for my anointed one.
^{18} His enemies I will clothe with disgrace,
     but on him, his crown will gleam."

CHAPTER THIRTEEN

JERUSALEM—GOD'S FOOTSTOOL

"Let us go to his dwelling place;
let us worship at his footstool."
Psalm 132:7

A t eighteen verses this Psalm of Ascent is the longest in the collection. It begins with the psalmist calling on God to remember David's vow to give the Ark of the Covenant a home. In chapter nine, we read about King David's restlessness that the ark, the symbol of God's presence, would have a place to reside. If David brought the ark to Jerusalem, God would bless the nation of Israel. David honored God by keeping his vow. Thus, the theme for Psalm 132 is if we honor God with our lives, He will honor us in return.[1] Like David, our lives must honor Christ and so closely abide in Him that it motivates us to accomplish God's will.[2] Here, in verse 1 our psalmist reiterates to God the priority of David's heart.

> O LORD, remember in David's favor all the hardships he endured; how he swore to the LORD and vowed to the Mighty One of Jacob, "I will not enter my house or get into my bed; I will not give sleep to my eyes or slumber to my eyelids, until I find a place for the LORD, a dwelling place for the Mighty One of Jacob" (Psalm 132:1-5).

David's desire was to bring honor to God by bringing the ark–at the time still in Jaar (v.6) which is the shortened name for Kiriath-jearim–to Jerusalem. "We heard of it in Ephrathah; we found it in the fields of Jaar." Recall that it was the object of a war trophy when the Philistines defeated Israel (1 Samuel 4) until it brought tragedy and was returned to Israel, to Kiriath-jearim where it remained until David went for it.

Because the pilgrims made annual journeys to Jerusalem, it seemed fitting that the ark's rightful home was Jerusalem–designated as God's footstool. "Let us go to his dwelling place; let us worship at his footstool" (v. 7). Jerusalem represents the footstool–an abstract concept that His spirit dwells at a site on earth. The metaphor conveys Him seated on a throne in heaven (Isaiah 6; Ezekiel 1; Revelation 4) and propping His feet on earth by way of the Ark of the Covenant.[3]

The Bible offers the foundational understanding why honoring God with our lives is so vital. First Corinthians 6:19 says, "Or do you not know that your body is a temple of the Holy Spirit within you, which

KEY POINT #1

Believers belong to Jesus and the goal of the believer's heart is to live to honor and please Him.

you have from God, and that you are not your own? For you were bought with a price; therefore glorify God in your body." When you became a Christ follower you surrendered your life and will for the life and will of Christ. The Holy Spirit took up residence within you. Christ's life now occupies your body, a temple for God's use—to honor and glorify Him. As believers, our bodies belong to God and we are commanded to not violate His standards for living.[4] Believers belong to Jesus and the goal of the believer's heart is to live to honor and please Him (Romans 14:7-8).

Today, the practice of honoring God is hard to find. Examples of dishonor are everywhere—on television, in newspapers, on the radio, and even in our neighborhoods. The Greek word for honor is *timao*, which means "to prize, i.e. fix a valuation upon, to revere."[5] Showing honor means treating those that we highly value with care. The Bible contains numerous stories of people who honored God with their hearts and actions. Yet, it doesn't conceal the stories of those whose hearts failed in this area. Malachi 3:6 says, "For I the LORD do not change." God still expects people to honor Him, and those in leadership roles to lead fairly with no tolerance for foul or obnoxious practices, such as what we'll read from the story of Eli today.

> **TODAY'S PEARL**
>
> "Teach me your way, O Lord, that I may walk in your truth; give me an undivided heart to revere your name" (Psalm 86:11).

Honor 101: What Honor Isn't

"For those who honor me I will honor" (1 Samuel 2:30). Those words spoken by a prophet were for the high priest Eli, after he failed miserably as a father. Eli's two disappointing sons, Hophni and

Phinehas, both whom held positions of honor, as priests failed to give God the utmost honor. "Now the sons of Eli were scoundrels; they had no regard for the LORD or for the duties of the priests to the people" (1 Samuel 2:12-13). Because of their pride, they misused their position as priests, mistreated people, and disregarded worship. Hophni and Phinehas didn't personally know God; their views of God were not shaped by Scripture (vv. 12-13). Eli was aware of the unacceptable behavior of his sons but failed to discipline them. He had a very common problem we see today. He poured his efforts into his job as a priest, but neglected to be the kind of parent his son's needed. The recognition and respect Eli attained in his professional life didn't extend to his handling of his home life.[6] By allowing his sons to carry on in sinful behavior, Eli was guilty of honoring his sons above God (v. 29). He failed to teach them to commit themselves to God first.

> **KEY POINT #2**
>
> For believers today, honoring the Lord comes by knowing Him personally.

Because God is just, He intervened with disciplinary actions. He will not overlook those who justify their own sin, as Eli may have done, thinking that as a religious leader God would somehow look the other way. "See, a time is coming when I will cut off your strength and the strength of your ancestor's family, so that no one in your family will live to old age" (v.31). And as for Eli's two sons? "The fate of your two sons, Hophni and Phinehas, shall be the sign to you–both of them shall die on the same day" (v. 34). God's pronouncement was fulfilled in 1 Kings 2:26. Solomon removed Abiathar from his position, thus ending Eli's line.[7]

For believers today, honoring the Lord comes only by knowing Him personally. This doesn't mean simply attaining head knowledge, which is void of a relationship, but in conjunction with developing and fostering an abiding bond with Jesus, our hearts grow in godly devotion. Arthur Pink makes this association from Eli's life:

> Those who give Him His proper place in their lives are richly rewarded here, as well as hereafter. God's dealings with us in this life are largely determined by the manner and measure in which we esteem and magnify Him.[8]

Honor God and He Will Honor You

In the book of Ezra, a second group of Babylonian exiles returned to Jerusalem. Ezra, a scribe among the exiles in Babylon, led this group of about 2000 men and their families.[9] Unlike Eli, Ezra gave God the proper place in his life. His priority was to live his life honoring and pleasing God. In order to return to Jerusalem, Ezra needed a decree from King Artaxerxes. God chose to honor Ezra by moving in the heart of King Artaxerxes (Ezra 7:6) who willingly gave Ezra the decree he needed. Long before God used Ezra to lead the second wave of exiles back to Jerusalem, He prepared him for this very task. As a scribe, he studied God's Word and obeyed its commands. He then dedicated himself to teaching them to God's people. It was through Ezra's teaching and his honorable actions that God blessed his efforts and honored him by making him an effective vessel to get God's people moving in the right direction spiritually.

KEY POINT #3

Even before we know in what capacity God will use us, it begins with a personal commitment to set our hearts on the path of honoring the Lord.

We don't have to become Bible teachers like Ezra in order to honor God, but we can follow his example by reading God's Word and fixing our hearts to living according to what His Word says. Even before we know in what capacity God will use us, it begins with a personal commitment to set our hearts on the path of honoring the Lord. God is always on the lookout for faithful hearts who want to serve and honor Him.

Men and Women of Honor Live by Faith

Our military's history is immersed in honor. All branches of the armed forces highly value this noble character trait. Honor is the overall means by which we measure the performance of our military. Qualities such as integrity, leading by example, doing the right thing, accountability, courage, strength, problem-solving, decisiveness, fitness, and others, encapsulate the grit of our military, and contributes to the end result of any mission. Add a faith in God to noble character and we have a powerful Advocate on our country's side. By valuing a high standard of moral character, we create and project a certain reputation–a reputation that must be upheld if our country is to continue to be a respected superpower.

Some would say that dismissing highly qualified military personnel due to their personal indiscretions does our military and country a disservice because we lose their skill, expertise, and experience. On the other side of this debate are those who believe that our country's integrity suffers when high ranking military members commit wrongdoings because it goes against the moral fabric of our country's values. Because of their irresponsible transgression, their focus and our country's priorities have been compromised, and it sets a bad precedent to those they lead.

I would be amiss if I didn't say that honor can't be compromised. It must be the military's highest benchmark. If this quality is the objective, our military will rise and maintain its military strength because it will be led by men and women of honor. Right beside honor is accountability. The interesting truth about accountability is that it leads to consequences–either good or bad. If we hold other governments accountable for how they govern their people, then America must also walk the talk and hold accountable those in high positions within our own governmental agencies, including our military. If we want to introduce positive changes and moral influence into other countries in a state of flux, accountability–with consequences–must start from our own top leaders. Otherwise, leaders with compromised lifestyles, opens the doors for others to deviate from the original moral standard.

Earlier, we read about how Eli, the high priest, who failed God in the parenting of his sons. He failed to honor God as a parent. God doesn't have two standards–one for work conduct and the other for personal conduct. Honor is all-inclusive. Eli was in that position by God's design, and He expected leaders to lead with upright living. The bottom line is that if God sees a high ranking official unable to honorably carry out his or her position, He has the right to find someone else to take their place. Honor has as much to do with how well we faithfully carry out our job duties as it does with our moral character.

Being a Christ follower, combined with military service, is highly regarded in the Bible. If this were not so, how could we explain the portrayal of David, also a soldier, as "having a heart after God"? And in Matthew 8:5-13 when Cornelius, the Roman centurion, approached Jesus and asked Him to heal his servant, Jesus didn't discourage Cornelius from having a career as a soldier.[11] Cornelius imparted personal integrity into his everyday duties. Even the Jews, who despised the Romans, respected this godly Gentile Roman soldier who honored God.

God Always Honors His Word

The remaining verses of Psalm 132 focus on the glorious outcome to the requests the psalmist presented in the first ten verses.

Rise up, O LORD, and go to your resting place, you and the ark of your might. Let your priests be clothed with righteousness, and let your faithful shout for joy. For your servant David's sake do not turn away the face of your anointed one (vv. 8-10).

Our psalmist invited the Lord to take His presence and power to the temple that was now finished. Those present for this momentous occasion prayed that the priests who would conduct the future worship services inside the new temple would be clothed in righteousness, and that they would be men of godly character. Even though David's descendants failed in keeping their end of the covenant many times (vv. 10-11), God still kept His promise as recorded in 2 Samuel 7. The psalmist now calls for God to fulfill that oath He made to David–a trumpet call for God to bring forth one of David's sons to the throne (v.11). For the psalmist, his chief interest was that God would preserve the family dynasty.

"There I will cause a horn to sprout up for David; I have prepared a lamp for my anointed one" (v. 17). The word **horn** used in this psalm represents strength. The psalmist is referring to the future son of David who would be their next king. However, it would ultimately be Jesus who would be that horn (representing strength, authority, and power) that would sprout up from David's line. The lamp, also mentioned in 1 Kings 11:36, is a biblical image. In a pagan world, the kings of David's line were to function as lamps to the nations.[10] Here again we see this metaphor to represent the shining light to be that of the coming of the Messiah.

"For the LORD has chosen Zion; he has desired it for his habitation" (v. 13). God has chosen Jerusalem as the manifestation of His presence. "This is my resting place forever; here I will reside, for I have desired it" (v. 14). The reference *my resting place* is a theme carried throughout the Bible with its New Testament emphasis on Jesus as the source of our rest (Matthew 11:28).

To be "clothed with salvation, and its faithful will shout for joy" (v.16) refers to believers. The illustration represents Christ's shed blood enveloping you, washing away all sin. Then, Jesus lovingly wraps His clothes made of heaven's warm salvation around you. This is certainly a cause for Christ's faithful ones to shout for joy. But those who are enemies of God will be fully clad in dishonor (v. 18).

David lived and breathed to glorify God and, likewise, when we do the same, God notices. Even if we fall short, like David, God is faithful to the promises He makes in His Word. Psalm 132 closes with the psalmist contemplating on that great day in Israel's history, remembering when the Ark of the Covenant was brought to Jerusalem. He links that grand event to praising God for the fulfillment of His oath to continue David's line.

Prayer for a Life that Honors God

Lord,

Help me to always keep my commitment to You–to live a life with actions and words that honor Your name. I honor You because You redeemed my life and gave me an eternal purpose. There is no other god worthy of my heart's devotion and allegiance. There is no other god who draws near when I am low. There is no other god who whispers, "I still love you, even when you fail. Keep going in my strength." There is no other God who can turn ashes from a broken life into a garment of beauty and praise (Isaiah 61:3). There is no other god who replaces my fears with godly hope. There is no other god who knows the wounds of my heart, but is the Lifter of my head (Psalm 3:3). When everything seems to be going against me, there is no other god that is still for me, but You, Lord.

You are highly exalted above all You've created. I exalt Your name because You are perfect in your actions, power, judgment, love, and mercy. Enable me to carry out my military duties in honorable service. And help me to never treat You so commonplace as to devalue Your exalted status, but to give You the proper place and position You deserve. Amen.

Key Points from Chapter 13

1. Believers belong to Jesus and the goal of the believer's heart is to live to honor and please Him.

2. For believers today, honoring the Lord comes by knowing Him personally.

3. Even before we know in what capacity God will use us, it begins with a personal commitment to set our hearts on the path of honoring the Lord.

Readers Reflections

1. What impression do you think people have of you by the way you honor them?

2. Are there any changes needed in order to make honoring Jesus a way of life?

3. Do you think the act of honoring someone or something has lost its original meaning or purpose as compared to 50 or 60 years ago?

Psalm of Strength

"Those who love me, I will deliver; I will protect those who know my name. When they call to me, I will answer them; I will be with them in trouble, I will rescue them and honor them" **(Psalm 91:14-15).**

PSALM OF ASCENT 133

[1] How very good and pleasant it is
    when kindred live together in unity!
[2] It is like the precious oil on the head,
    running down upon the beard,
    on the beard of Aaron,
    running down over the collar of his robes.
[3] It is like the dew of Hermon,
    which falls on the mountains of Zion.
    For there the LORD ordained his blessing,
    life forevermore.

THE OIL THAT UNIFIES AND THE DEW THAT BLESSES

How very good and pleasant it is
when kindred live together in unity!
Psalm 133:1

How would you describe your relationship with your siblings while growing up? Were they harmonious relationships, or were they tension filled with impatience, constant bickering, jealousy, or outbursts of anger? Did your parents foster unity with well-balanced rules and respect for one another, sprinkled with memorable experiences of lighthearted fun and family outings? Were they united in one accord in creating stable childhoods for you and your siblings? And if adversity or difficult times arrived at the door of your childhood home, how did your family react? Did these family struggles strengthen your family bond or pull your family further apart?

Our fourteenth Psalm of Ascent is centered on the necessity of unity within our families. This Psalm of Ascent, the last one written by David, was all too familiar with family conflict. The writer probably appreciated periods of unity simply because he experienced the heartache family discord creates. Perhaps he was in one such season of unity when he penned the first verse of this psalm: "How very good and pleasant it is when kindred live together in unity."

Problems Behind Palace Doors

King David was a far better ruler than he was a parent. He deliberately planted the seed of sin that triggered a string of horrific consequences for himself and his family. Trouble–the kind that originates from within the family and caused by the sin of a single member–can bring on catastrophic consequences. Selfishness, parental irresponsibility, uncontrolled anger, abuse, disrespect, infidelity, and other problems bring unforeseeable consequences which, sadly, can linger for decades, or even a lifetime. We rarely come out unscathed. The innocent victims can wind up hurt, broken, embittered, or even estranged.

KEY POINT #1

While God does forgive sin, it doesn't necessarily mean He cancels sin's consequences.

David brought turmoil upon his household when he sinned with Bathsheba. Then to cover up his misdeed he had Bathsheba's husband, Uriah killed in battle. Because he "utterly scorned the LORD" (2 Samuel 12:14) God set forth His judgment on David.

> Now therefore the sword shall never depart from your house, for you have despised me, and have taken the wife of Uriah

the Hittite to be your wife. I will raise up trouble against you from within your own house; and I will take your wives before your eyes, and give them to your neighbor, and he shall lie with your wives in the sight of this very sun. For you did it secretly; but I will do this thing before all Israel, and before the sun (2 Samuel 12:10-12).

David sinned in private, but God's disciplinary action was public. Even today we see examples of public discipline. Citizens who serve the public, and who are caught up in personal indiscretions or criminal behavior, all too often find themselves portrayed in a humiliating light by the media for all to see. This is called a reproof—being exposed or singled out in public. The word reproof has the idea of testing something to expose its true nature.[1] It's proving the inner reality in order to bring to light any flaws or mistakes.[2] Briefly, to reprove is to expose.[3]

David's position as king had no bearing on God's punishment on him. David had abused his position of authority. While God does forgive sin, this doesn't necessarily mean He cancels sin's consequences. His just and righteous nature requires punishment. Galatians 6:7-8 says, "Do not be deceived; God is not mocked, for you reap whatever you sow. If you sow to your own flesh, you will reap corruption from the flesh; but if you sow to the Spirit, you will reap eternal life from the Spirit."

The consequences God handed down to David came to pass. David contended with threats of murder in his family, and he saw how his mistakes as a father surfaced in his own children's lives. His son, Absalom would later rebel against his father by plotting to overthrow him.[4] David also had to confront sexual sins within his own family. His other son, Amnon raped his half sister, Tamar. Then two years later, still angry and bitter, Absalom took revenge and murdered Amnon for violating his sister. While David was unrivaled as a king and military leader, he lacked the ability to be an effective parent. It is easy to see why the home of the royal family was rarely a harmonious one.

Nonetheless, God forgave David, but He didn't remove the consequences. And sadly, some of these consequences affected innocent people. Charles R. Swindoll says in his book, *A Man of Passion and Destiny: David*, "It is those domestic consequences that create what has become to be known as dysfunctional families."[5]

The Oil that Unifies

David uses the metaphor of oil to describe how precious unity is, whether in the church or in our homes. "It [unity] is like the precious oil on the head, running down upon the beard, on the beard of Aaron, running down over the collar of his robes" (v. 2). Oil is a symbol of the Holy Spirit. Its purpose is to bless someone for a particular calling. In Leviticus 8:12 oil was used in blessing Aaron for his role as high priest. "He poured some of the anointing oil on Aaron's head and anointed him, to consecrate him." Others who were also anointed with oil were the kings of Israel and some of the prophets (1 Kings 19:16). Mark 14 tells the story of Mary anointing Jesus before His death. Once the jar of perfume was broken open, its sweet fragrance filled the air. In the same way, when God's children live in harmonious relationships, their homes are blessed with the sweet fragrance of unity.

KEY POINT #2

Spiritual unity serves a valuable purpose within the body of believers, but when unity is present in your military home, it is like the anointing oil that unifies, building resilience for times of severe trials or adversity.

Spiritual unity serves a valuable purpose within the body of believers, but when unity is present in your military home, it's like the anointing oil that unifies, building resilience for times of severe trials or adversity.

The energy, devotion, and commitment emitted from a family united in one accord reinforce family bonds. Just as the military has implemented programs for service members to help them adjust and move forward after major setbacks, the military family is supported with a variety of services geared to building resiliency.

Unity in the military family also functions much like a team and, like the military, it should leave no member alone. When Jesus agonized in the garden about his impending trial and death, He referred to the coming agony and separation from his heavenly Father as the "cup." "Father, if you are willing, remove this cup from me; yet, not my will but yours be done" (Luke 22:43). God didn't remove Jesus' suffering, but He did send an angel to strengthen Him. God is relational and because He wired us to also be relational, we have a built-in need to be in meaningful and healthy relationships. Fellow Christians are God's agents to come alongside believers during difficult times to comfort, strengthen, support, and encourage. "For where two or three are gathered in my name,

> **KEY POINT #3**
>
> If the strong bond of unity is the spiritual rhythm of your military family, God is in its midst, and His strength empowers your family to better cope with future trials or difficult circumstances.

I am there among them" (Matthew 18:20). At no other time does the spiritual unity of believers soothe and comfort more than during times of deep distress.

Furthermore, Christians are encouraged to bring their most difficult struggles and setbacks to their church for God's guidance in seeking spiritual solutions and biblical support. Spiritual unity is one of the important roles of the Holy Spirit.[6] Think of spiritual unity as a form of life insurance. If you are an active participant in a local church and you have made spiritual investments into that body of believers, you have many spiritual resources from which to draw if a crisis or a severe hardship hits your family. This body is your spiritual family and they pay wonderful dividends in the form of spiritual wisdom, support and encouragement. God has a special way of taking your struggle, and finding another believer who has experienced the same or a similar hardship who can now come alongside you.

> **KEY POINT #4**
>
> Disunity steals the spiritual energy of the home and is the work of Satan. He uses disunity to bring division.

Your spiritual family members add additional muscle to your family's resiliency. If the strong bond of unity is the spiritual rhythm of your military family, God is in its midst, and His strength empowers your family to better cope with future trials or difficult circumstances.

That being said, if the brutal realities of life common to the military lifestyle touch your family with combat stress, or posttraumatic stress disorder (PTSD), thoughts of suicide, difficult children's issues, problems with transitioning, domestic violence, and other concerns in which your family has been greatly impacted, I encourage you to take a vital step and contact one of the various programs uniquely tailored to the needs of today's military family. If there is a deep throbbing agony in your heart, getting the targeted help and support your family needs is being attentive and responsible to the emotional, physical, and spiritual needs of your family. There's no shame in seeking services when it comes to the well-being of your family. Billy Graham once said, "Apart from religious influence, the family is the most important unit of society."

Conversely, if disunity gets a foothold, we'll find ourselves in spiritual warfare with the devil. As with any war, we need to know our enemy and how to fight him. God has provided us with tools to combat Satan. If we don't use the principles of God's armor found in Ephesians 6, Satan will use what is already a weak link. Because we are on the Lord's side, Satan uses division in a family to steal the spiritual energy of the home. If we allow him to win in that area, we put our family resiliency at risk for enduring difficult times. We need the supernatural power of the Holy Spirit working God's strength inside our hearts and minds. With the additional backing of God's armor, you and your family are well protected and prepared for battle.

Solomon says in Ecclesiastes 4:12, "Though one might prevail against another, two will withstand one. A threefold cord is not quickly broken." The Christian community recognizes this verse referring to marriage, but it can also be applied to your military home. Angela Smith, in an online article, called "The Power of a Three-Stranded Cord in an Unequal Marriage," gives us an example of how this concept works.

> The illustration of the three-stranded cord…though makes even more sense when you speak to a rope maker. They will tell you that this is the strongest cord you can make because all three strands are touching each other. If you add more strands, the rope becomes thicker but not necessarily stronger because not all the strands are touching at the same time. If one or even two of the strands becomes frayed or broken, the cord will remain intact as long as the third strand does not break. [7]

If you substitute yourself and your spouse as being one strand, and your children as the second, with God being the third, when adversity comes, as long as the third strand doesn't break, your family will remain intact. God may permit some pain and suffering in the struggle, but He'll be the strength that sustains your family. He made us to be in harmonious families, working together to build one another up. Sharing life's most difficult challenges as harmonious family members brings relief and perseverance that isolation and discord can't offer. And since God is not breakable, His strength sustains the military family through a season of adversity. During this time, the two strands–represented by the parents and the children–draw closer together, with God at the center empowering all three cords.

Unity Multiplies

We can take the metaphor of the oil poured over Aaron's head one step further. The second half of verse 2–"running down upon the beard, on the beard of Aaron, running down over the collar of his robes"– symbolizes unity in a broader form. A family that has established a solid presence of spiritual unity is contagious, with a strong potential of spreading to other family members. The entire family unit is blessed with the sanctification of the anointing oil of unity.[8] When the children marry, they become agents of harmony themselves, imparting his or her own sweet aroma of unity into their own families. The strong bond of unity expressed in your home is a powerful witness for the Lord, especially in light of the high divorce rate among military marriages.

The Dew that Blesses

There is a rather interesting geography lesson in the metaphor in verse 3. Our psalmist compares unity to the "dew of Hermon, which falls on the mountains of Zion." Mount Hermon, the highest mountain in that part of the world, is located north of Israel.[9] Its height is over 9,000 feet.[10] The early morning dew that descends overnight and rests on campers who have pitched a tent near its summit experience the uncomfortable feeling of waking up drenched.[11] Mount Zion, (Jerusalem), however, reaches to a height of only about 2,400 feet.[12] Yet, the morning dew manufactured over Mt. Hermon falls on both. Even though it isn't clearly known why this happens, nonetheless, it provides the needed moisture for the crops during the dry season.

God's desire has always been to bestow blessings on His people. The ancient nation of Israel struggled to maintain unity, while at the same time they seldom experienced His blessings due to their disobedience. With the division of the two kingdoms—the northern kingdom of Israel and the southern kingdom of Judah—the metaphor further illustrates how our psalmist longed for unity to exist and bless the people of both kingdoms.

The overarching premise of this metaphor is the image that the morning dew evokes of unity—kindred getting along. Unity to overcome adversity can't flow in the absence of unconditional love. Eugene Peterson explains, "When we are in a community with those Christ loves and redeems, we are constantly finding out new things about them."[13] Like the dew that is new every morning, harmonious relationships blessed with unity grow in spiritual understanding, and we learn from one another new truths about our faith in Christ. Unity is a key component in the life of a believer. Without it, the love of Christ within us might go unnoticed by the world.

One of my favorite quotes comes from Soren Kierkegaard. "Life must be lived forward; it can only be understood backwards." Whether your childhood included a harmonious family life or not, when you look at your family experiences with a backward glance you realize, perhaps with children of your own, God offers a second chance of pursuing a spirit of family unity. This doesn't just happen; it has to be pursued then maintained. Ephesians 3:3 says, "…making every effort to maintain the unity of the Spirit in the bond of peace." When there is a genuine spirit of unity in the home there is a spirit of peace as well. We must have the spirit of Christ living in–and working through–us in order for unity to put its roots down deep. It requires sowing the seed of unity in order to reap a harvest of harmony in both our earthly and spiritual families.

Prayer for Unity and Harmony in Our Homes and Lives

Lord,

As creator of heaven and earth, it was Your original intent that all You created were to live in unity and in harmony. However, sin has scarred Your creation. Much of the world today seems to lack any spiritual rhythm or harmony. The world is divided–wars and civil wars abound, governments and people disagree, and cultural and racial tensions continue to divide us. Even Christian homes are struggling to keep the world's negative influences from causing strife and discord.

Lord, I bring to You each of my family relationships. Move in their hearts a desire to "put away all bitterness and wrath and anger and wrangling and slander, together with all malice, and be kind to one another, tenderhearted, forgiving one another" (Ephesians 4:31-32). Break down any walls that have become barriers to establishing unity and heal our hearts. Help us to live and walk in agreement with one another (Amos 3:3). Let harmony be the rhythm that unites us, building strength and developing resiliency. Make our bond strong like the strength of a three-strand cord, not easily broken. Protect our home, Lord, and fill it with the fragrance of unity and the blessing of harmonious relationships.

Lord, thank you for each of my spiritual friendships. Your Word says in Proverbs 13:20, "Whoever walks with the wise becomes wise, but the companion of fools suffers harm." Because bad friendships can cause us to compromise our morals, protect my family's spiritual relationships from any form of deception or division.

Like the metaphor of the dew falling on both Mount Hermon and Mount Zion, let the spirit of unity descend upon both my physical and spiritual families. May we remain in one accord, "clothing ourselves with love, which binds everything together in perfect harmony" (Colossians 3:14). Amen.

Chapter Fourteen Key Points

1. While God does forgive sin, it doesn't necessarily mean He cancels sin's consequences.
2. Spiritual unity serves a valuable purpose within the body of believers, but when unity is present in your military home, it is like the anointing oil that unifies, building resilience for times of severe trials or adversity.
3. If the strong bond of unity is the spiritual rhythm of your military family, God is in its midst, and His strength empowers your family to better cope with future trials or difficult circumstances.
4. Disunity steals the spiritual energy of the home and is the work of Satan. He uses disunity to bring division.

Reader's Reflections

1. Describe an experience when you distinctly felt the warm and soothing friendship of spiritual unity of a fellow believer(s)?
2. Did you perceive a spiritual rhythm in your childhood home? If so, describe what it was like. If not, does the absence of a spiritual rhythm prompt you to build spiritual unity in your home now?
3. What are the pieces of God's armor and their purposes? See Ephesians 6.

Psalm of Strength

"May God be gracious to us and bless us and make his face to shine upon us, that your way may be known upon earth, your saving power among all nations. Let the peoples [in unity] praise you, O God; let all the peoples praise you"

(Psalm 67:1-3).

PSALMS OF ASCENT 134

[1] Come, bless the LORD, all you servants
of the LORD,
who stand by night in the house of the
LORD!
[2] Lift up your hands to the holy place,
and bless the LORD.
[3] May the LORD, maker of heaven and earth,
bless you from Zion.

GOD BLESSES THOSE WHO BLESS HIM

Lift up your hands to the holy place, and bless the Lord.
Psalm 134:2

L ike Psalm 133, this final Psalm of Ascent is three short verses that call our attention to the word *bless*. But before we discover the significance of this word that embodies this psalm, let's reflect a moment on the journey of these resolute pilgrims. We joined them in Psalm 120, the starting point of their trek through unfamiliar territory and heathen people, making them feel vulnerable to attack. Often walking at night to avoid the heat of the day, they depended upon the Lord to be their Keeper. While navigating through the menacing mountains, they maintained their focus upwards trusting God as their Source of help. They sang of God's tireless care and recounted the times that if it had not been for the Lord they would have been annihilated by their enemies. In Psalm 126, they recounted how God freed their ancestors from decades of captivity, turning their tears of sorrow into harvests of joy. In the middle of their journey, perhaps families comingled and swapped stories common to their way of life. They feared the Lord and understood that unless He was the foundation of their homes and lives, their endeavors were futile. They praised God for His love that strengthens and protects and in Psalm 130 rejoiced over His declaration of mercy and forgiveness. In Psalm 132, God did more than just promise to continue David's dynasty, He promised all mankind a Savior who would reign forever.

KEY POINT #1

To bless is to ask God to bring about a desired result, either something tangible or intangible from something else.

And so we come to Psalm 134 culminating with the pilgrims ascending Mount Zion (Jerusalem) to worship the Lord one final time. The first verse begins with, "Come, bless the LORD, all you servants of the LORD, who stand by night in the house of the Lord!"

The word *bless* means "to speak well of or approve."[1] And the word *blessing* means "the act or words of one that blesses."[2] Our psalmist uses the word *bless* in a dual fashion—*from* our heavenly Father, and *to* our heavenly Father. But what does it mean to request a blessing from God? When we sit down for a meal we ask God to bless the food, to bless our home, our lives, our military, and our country. But when we ask Him to bless these things, what are we really asking Him to do?

To request a blessing from God is to ask Him to bring about a desired result, either something tangible or intangible from something else. If we're about to embark on a mission trip, we ask God to bless our efforts—that our good works will produce fruit that glorifies God. If we ask God to bless our jobs, we desire Him

---

KEY POINT #2

To bless God is to
communicate our devotion
to Him by praising Him
with loving sentiments and
through caring actions
towards others that reflect
His importance and value in
our lives.

---

to enable us to do our best
work, to have favor with our
employer. If we ask God to bless
our military, we pray for their
protection from our enemies;
godly decisions by leadership;
wisdom and understanding of
our enemy's motives and tactics;
and guidance and protection for
their families. If you ask God to bless your marriage, you pray that
He'll bless your union and deepen your love for one another. The
more specific our requests for His blessing, the better our ability
to ascertain the degree to which He has blessed us in that request.
Asking God to bless the important areas of our lives tells Him that
we desire Him to be divinely involved.

Bless the Lord in the Night

Psalm 134 begins with "Come, bless the LORD." In many of the
Psalms of Ascents, the writers requested something of God, but here
in this final psalm, the writer instructs the pilgrims to do the only
appropriate thing–to instead bless the Lord. It is a proper conclusion
to the festival–blessing the Lord in remembrance of His role as the
great Overseer of their lives. Since we cannot bless God with anything
tangible, our only means of doing so is by intangible measures. We
do that by communicating our devotion to Him by praising Him
with loving sentiments and through caring actions towards others that
reflect His importance and value in our lives. Our sentiments float up
to heaven and bless the heart of God. Other ways to bless Him are by
giving thanks through the act of taking communion, extending grace
to others, by the way we live, making godly choices, and having an
attitude of gratitude.

Verse 1 opens with a moving invitation, but to who isn't entirely known. A little temple history will help clarify the meaning of "who stand by night in the house of the Lord."

The Levite priests were the ministers of their day. They pointed Israel to God. In addition to being in charge of the worship services in the temple, they were also responsible for the temple's safety, never leaving it vulnerable.[3] Like the night watchmen who stood on the walls protecting the city within, the temple priests stood watch day and night to protect the temple from raids and pillage.[4] The Israelites viewed all aspects of the priest's work as an act of praise to God, done well and reverently.[5]

It's highly probable that this invitation to "all you servants of the LORD, who stand by night in the house of the Lord!" may have been said "by the watch going off duty to the priests who would relieve them; the latter group responding with the benediction, 'May the Lord, the Maker of heaven and earth, bless you from Zion.'"[6] Another possibility is that it was a morning greeting "between the congregation assembled on the hill of the Lord and the priests who had charge of the night watch."[7]

The nights were quiet as one would expect of a temple. Remaining alert with an attitude of worship was probably the watchers' nightly nemesis. Perhaps the high priests in charge were responsible for the nightly reveille for the temple priests to worship the Lord in the wee hours of the night as a means to fight off drowsiness.[8] By definition, worship is appreciating God for

TODAY'S PEARL

"I will call to mind the deeds of the LORD; I will remember your wonders of old. I will meditate on all your work, and muse on your mighty deeds. Your way, O God, is holy. What god is so great as our God? You are the God who works wonders; you have displayed your might among the peoples" (Psalm 77:11-14).

His nature and His worth,[9] and it was an integral part of the ancient Israelites' lives. The priests labored a great deal in preparing for worship so that the pilgrims who entered could immediately focus their hearts and minds on God.

Today, busy families often rush into church services without any preparation of the heart. We settle into our pew and before long our thoughts drift to the activities and concerns of the coming week. Our focus is out of alignment. First Corinthians 14:40 says, "all things should be done decently and in order." That means God desires our time of worship to be methodical with structure and direction so our hearts are prepared for hearing from Him. We are then mindful of God's presence in our lives and His sovereignty over our circumstances. Genuine worship then becomes the focus of our lives on a daily basis not just an hour each Sunday.[10]

The pilgrims responded to the call to exalt their God. In spiritual unity, they lifted their hands and blessed the Lord. These were people just like us, with difficult seasons and just as many concerns, and also fiercely hated. And yet they praised Him in the night as well as in the day. Have you ever been troubled by something so worrisome that it kept you up at night? It is during these dark nights of our soul that in our crying out to the Lord, we should also offer up a sacrifice of praise. In the midst of our debilitating pain, He receives our praises, knowing it's freely offered from the pit of our crushed soul. When we bless God, He blesses us.

Our study of King Jehoshaphat in chapter 2 is a vivid example of a man who blessed the heart of God and in return God blessed the king during a time of great distress. In seeking God's help to fight multiple armies bearing down on his kingdom, the king called his people to a period of fasting. He acknowledged before God His power, recollected His past help, and the king's dependence on Him. These praises were blessings directed at God, and He responded with a blessing of His own–bringing victory to the king's army. God blesses those who bless Him.

Bombarded by worrisome circumstances of weary believers today, we can find ourselves looking at worship from the standpoint of simply filling our emotional and spiritual tanks. More often than we realize, we arrive at church seeking only to be blessed. Although this is part of the worship experience and a function of churches today, it shouldn't be the exclusive motive of our hearts. Jesus was a servant-not a taker, but a giver. Simply viewing worship from the standpoint of what it will do for us, and not blessing in return, is to miss out on the spiritual harvest of fulfilling His purposes for our lives. Additionally, if the motive of our hearts is merely to gain a benefit like securing a business connection, establishing a social network, or being in the right church circles, our understanding of worship is skewed. Eugene H. Peterson, translator of *The Message,* says, "You are here [in church] because God blessed you. Now you bless God."[11]

Our Marching Orders to Bless

By the same measure we come to worship to seek the Lord's blessing for our own life journeys, we are to praise God for what He has accomplished in and through us. We have nothing to give God that He can't get for Himself, but the longing of His heart is to hear our praises. A heartfelt "thank you" will go a long way with God. Believers who appreciate the Lord as the great Keeper and Overseer of their lives, and acknowledge His handiwork have plenty of reasons for blessing the Lord. Walter C. Kaiser said, "People who praise little, or not at all, grow small in their thinking and living for God."[12]

KEY POINT #3

We have nothing to give God that He can't get for Himself, but the longing of His heart is to hear our praises.

Unless God has revealed His will and plan for you to leave the service of your country, He has much to accomplish through you. He has called you to serve with a dual purpose. With the light of Christ as a hopeful beacon in a world filled with conflicts, civil wars and terrorism concerns, you are an agent of the Lord's with marching orders of a higher kind. Like the temple priests, you are a commissioned vessel God has equipped for service to this country and to glorify Him through it. Whatever your rank, when your military service is done responsibly and reverently, it becomes an act of blessing God and reflects proudly on your country. Like the temple priests who honored God by the quality of their work and the attitude of service they brought to it,[13] you and your family can be that lamp, that light, identifying God as the source of all your blessings—the very reason an unbeliever might inquire about your faith and resiliency. Faith makes a difference, providing the needed grit to carry on. A life blessing God pays wonderful dividends.

The Psalms of Ascent reveal that one of God's goals is to bring believers to a deeper level of worship of Him. Each psalm is a step—a testimony of the Israelites growing in their worship and trust of God, so you and I can appreciate, understand, and experience His blessings in a fuller measure.

Whether you're called to serve in the armed forces, or to a supportive role, God desires that we take the next steps of our own personal faith journeys. As we saw with the pilgrims, every step of their journey was a step taken in faith. They returned home blessed and their faith enriched. We, too, have the confidence of knowing that just as God was with them on their challenging trek, He is with us as we step into the future of our own journeys with God. The time has come to lift our hands and voices to bless God for His work here on earth. When we bless the Lord while performing the work He has assigned us, His blessing and favor return to us, our homes, our nation, and those who serve to protect her (Psalm 5:11-12). It is in this context that we arrive at our final verse of Psalm 134: "May the Lord, maker of heaven and earth, bless you from Zion."

Prayer for a Deeper Level of Worship

Lord,

I can't think of any action on my part as important as worshipping and blessing You. When I praise You, Your Holy Spirit's presence softens and shapes my heart and mind for Your purposes.

On days when things go wrong or when I'm in a trial that has me feeling beat up it is hard to bless You with devoted words. Forgive me when I fail to bless Your name when it is called for. Strengthen me to simply praise You even when I don't feel like it. For this reason, I am thankful that You are "gracious and merciful, slow to anger and abounding in steadfast love" (Psalm 145:8). Show me new ways to worship You so that my faith and devotion to You deepens.

Your Word is rich in meaning, understanding, and application. Thank You for showing me Your nature through Your Word. "Because Your steadfast love is better than life, my lips will praise You. So, I will bless you as long as I live; I will lift up my hands and call on your name" (Psalm 63:3-4). Thank You, Lord, that You are my Savior, my Helper, my Keeper, Comforter, Provider, and so much more. "But let all who take refuge in you rejoice; let them ever sing for joy. Spread your protection over them, so that those who love your name may exult in you. For you bless the righteous, O Lord; you cover them with favor as with a shield" (Psalm 5:11-12).

Lord, when I bless You, I am blessed in return. Let my life be a blessing to You. Let my words of devotion put a smile in Your heart. May all my deeds be motivated by a desire to exalt You. Amen.

Chapter 15 Key Points

1. To bless is to ask God to bring about a desired result, either something tangible or intangible from something else.

2. To bless God is to communicate our devotion to Him by praising Him with loving sentiments and through caring actions towards others that reflect His importance and value in our lives.

3. We have nothing to give God that He can't get for Himself, but the longing of His heart is to hear our praises.

Reader's Reflections

1. What about you? Has your manner of blessing the Lord through worship grown as a result of your journey through the Psalms of Ascent?

2. In general, has your understanding of the Psalms of Ascent broadened your understanding of the faith of the ancient Israelites?

3. What will your next step of faith look like as a result of reading this book?

Psalm of Strength

"Those who bring thanksgiving as their sacrifice honor me; to those who go the right way I will show the salvation of God"
(Psalm 50:23).

ABOUT THE AUTHOR

Lisa Nixon Phillips, a native of Lawrence, Kansas, met her husband, Ray, a machinist mate in the U.S. Navy in 1986. The following year they married. Lisa, a passionate supporter of her husband's military service, volunteered for various military family events during the span of her husband's 21 years of service. While stationed on the island of Guam, she served as an Ombudsman to the navy's ship repair facility.

Drawing from her love for God's Word and her 17 years as a military wife, Lisa's desire is to encourage current military families by applying the Scriptures to experiences and issues common to the military lifestyle. Her belief that faith makes a difference contributes to the spiritual readiness necessary to have a strong and resilient military family. Lisa's story, "The Fabric of a Seasoned Navy Wife," appeared in the 2008 edition of *A Cup of Comfort for Military Families–Stories that Celebrate Heroism on the Home Front.* She has also written for an online magazine for military wives called, *Wives in Bloom,* as well as a short narrative in *Military Lifestyle* magazine and an anthology titled "*Always Waiting Pier Side.*" After her husband's retirement, Lisa led a women's ministry in her church while working alongside her husband as the bookkeeper of their business, Ed's Transmission Exchange in Marysville, Washington. Lisa is a member of Blue Star Mothers, a non-profit organization for mothers with children serving in the armed forces. She and her husband now live in Arlington, Washington, and have two children. Her daughter, Megan, is married and serves as a first lieutenant in the Army National Guard. Her son, Lawrence, is a senior in high school and hopes to follow in his dad's footsteps and join the Navy upon graduation.

Contacting Lisa

If you have been touched by something you read in this book, or if you would like to read articles on the Psalms of Ascent that pertain to the military lifestyle, go to www.lisanixonphillips.com. Or by email at info@lisaphillips.com. And add me as a friend on Facebook: facebook.com/faithstepsformilitaryfamilies

END NOTES

Introduction
[1] Walter C. Kaiser, Jr., *The Journey Isn't Over* (Grand Rapids, MI: Baker Book House, 1993), 16.
[2] Bible Note for 2 Kings 20:11, *The Life Application Bible* (Iowa Falls, IA: World Bible Publisher, Inc., 1989).
[3] Bible Study Note for 2 Kings 20:8-11, *The English Standard Version*, (Wheaton, IL: Crossway, 2008).
[4] Kaiser, 16.
[5] Kings 20:8-11, *The English Standard Version*.

Chapter One
[1] James Strong, S.T.D. The *New Strong's Complete Dictionary of Bible Words* (Nashville, TN: Thomas Nelson Publishers, 1996), 11
[2] Bible Note for Psalm 120:5-6, *The Life Application Bible* (Iowa Falls, IA: World Bible Publishers, Inc., 1989).
[3] Ibid.
[4] Exodus 20:16, *Nelson's New King James Version* (Nashville, TN: Thomas Nelson Publishers, 1997).
[5] Ibid.
[6] Bible Note for Exodus 20:16, *The Life Application Bible*.
[7] Bible Note for Proverbs 21:6, *Nelson's New King James Version*.
[8] R. Tuck, "Coals of Juniper," 2010, http://www.ibiblestudies.com/auth/tuck/coals_of_juniper.htm (accessed 15 February 2013).
[9] Ibid.
[10] Ibid.

Chapter Two
[1] Study Notes for 2 Kings 5:2, *The Life Application Bible* (Iowa Falls, IA: World Bible Publishers, Inc.,1989).
[2] Study Notes for 2 Chronicles, The Blueprint, *The Life Application Bible*.
[3] Study Notes for 2 Chronicles 20:16–17, *The English Standard Version*, (Wheaton, IL: Crossway, 2008).

[4] David Jeremiah. *What in the World is Going On?* (Nashville, TN: Thomas Nelson Publishers, 2008), 127.

[5] *The New Strong's Complete Dictionary of Bible Words* (Nashville, TN: Thomas Nelson Publishers, 1996), 541.

Chapter Three

[1] Charles F. Stanley. *The Glorious Journey* (Nashville, TN: Thomas Nelson Publishers, 1996), 13.

[2] Rick Warren. The Purpose Driven Life (Grand Rapids, MI: Zondervan, 2002), 134.

[3] Ibid., 137.

[4] *Merriam-Webster's Collegiate Dictionary,* Eleventh Edition, s.v. (Springfield, MA: Merriam-Webster, Inc., 2005).

[5] Stanley, 13.

[6] Ibid.

[7] Bible Note for Revelation 3:20, *Life Application Bible* (Iowa Falls, IA: World Bible Publishers, Inc.,1989).

[8] Ibid.

[9] Bible Note for Leviticus 23:1, *Life Application Bible.*

[10] Ibid.

[11] Bible Note for Deuteronomy 17:8, *Life Application Bible.*

[12] Ibid.

Chapter Four

[1] *Merriam-Webster's Collegiate Dictionary*, Eleventh Edition, s.v. (Springfield, MA: Merriam-Webster, Inc., 2005).

[2] Bible Note for 1Samuel 5:1, *Life Application Bible* (Iowa Falls, IA: World Bible Publishers, Inc., 1989).

[3] Bible Note for 2 Samuel 6:20, *Life Application Bible.*

[4] Ibid.

[5] Ibid.

[6] Bible Note for Psalm 123:2, *Nelson's New King James Version* (Nashville, TN: Thomas Nelson Publishers, 1997).

[7] Don Burleson, "Familiarity Breeds Contempt," http://www.dba-oracle.com/t_familiarity_breeds_contempt.htm (accessed 15 April 2013).

[8] Rod Powers, "When Does Friendship Become a Crime in the Army? Army Fraternization Policy," http://www.usmilitary.about.com/od/army/a/fraternization.-u3q.htm. (accessed 27 March 2013).

[9] Ibid.

Chapter Five

[1] Beth Moore. *Stepping Up: A Journey through the Psalms of Ascent* (Nashville, TN: LifeWay Press, 2007), 55.

[2] Ibid. 54.

[3] Henry Ford, "Other Prominent Men Encourage," What Christians Want to Know, www.whatchristianswanttoknow.com/words-of-encouragement (accessed April 9, 2013).

[5] Bible Note for 1 Chronicles 16:7-36, *Life Application Bible* (Iowa Falls, IA: World Bible Publishers, Inc., 1989).

[6] Eugene H. Peterson. *A Long Obedience in the Same Direction* (Downers Grove, IL, InterVarsity Press, 2000), 79.

[7] Ibid. 79.

[8] Ibid. 79.

Chapter Six

[1] Bible Note for 2 Samuel 5:7, *Life Application Bible* (Iowa Falls, IA: World Bible Publishers, Inc., 1989).

[2] Ibid.

[3] Ibid.

[4] R.Leighton. *Streams in the Desert* (Grand Rapids, MI: Zondervan, 1997), 53.

[5] Bible Note for Psalm 125:1-2, *English Standard Version Study Bible* (Wheaton, IL.: Crossway, 2008).

[6] Ibid.

[7] Ibid.

[8] Walter C. Kaiser, Jr. *The Journey Isn't Over* (Grand Rapids, MI: Baker Book House, 1993), 70.

[9] Bible Note for Psalm 125:4-5, *English Standard Version Study Bible.*

Chapter Seven

[1] Bible Note for Ezra 1:1, *Life Application Bible* (Iowa Falls, IA: World Bible Publishers, Inc., 1989).

[2] Ibid.

[3] James Limburg, quoted in: Moore, Beth. *Steppin Up: A journey through the Psalms of Ascent* (Nashville, TN., Lifeway, 2008) p.76.

[4] Bible Note for Psalm 126:6, *Life Application Bible.*

[5] Bible Note for Job 42:10-11, *Life Application Bible.*

[6] Ibid.

Chapter Eight

[1] Walter C. Kaiser, Jr. *The Journey Isn't Over* (Grand Rapids, MI: Baker Book House Company, 1993), 82.

[2] Bible Note for 1 Chronicles 28:19, *Nelson's New King James Version* (Nashville, TN: Thomas Nelson Publishers, 1997.

[3] Bible Note for Psalm 127:1, *Life Application Bible* (Iowa Falls, IA: World Bible Publishers, Inc. 1989).

[4] Keith Krell, "Works:Purified or Fried?" Bible.org, www.bible.org/seriespage/works-purified-or-fried-1-corinthians-39-15.com. (accessed 27 April 2013)

[5] Bible Note for Matthew 7:24, *Nelson's New King James Version.*

[6] Beth Moore. *Stepping Up: A Journey through the Psalms of Ascent* (Nashville, TN: LifeWay, 2007), 87.

[7] *Merriam-Webster's Collegiate Dictionary*, Eleventh Edition, s.v. (Springfield, MA: Merriam-Webster, Inc., 2005).

[8] Bible Note for Psalm 127:5, *Nelson's New King James Version*

[9] Ibid.

[10] Bible Note for Psalm 127:5, *Nelson's New King James Version.*

Chapter Nine

[1] Eugene H. Peterson. *A Long Obedience in the Same Direction* (Downers Grove, IL, InterVarsity Press, 2000), 122.

[2] Study Notes for Romans 8:1 *The English Standard Version* (Wheaton, IL: Crossway, 2008).

[3] James Strong, LL.D., S.T.D. *The New Strong's Complete Dictionary of Bible Words* (Nashville, TN: Thomas Nelson Publishers, 1996), 532.

[4] Gene Taylor, "Reverence in Worship" http://www.centervilleroad.com/articles/reverence.html (accessed 9 May 2013).

[5] Bible Note for Matthew 8:8-12, *Life Application Bible* (Iowa Falls, IA: World Bible Publishers, Inc., 1989).

[6] Ibid.

[7] Bible Note for Psalm 97:10, *Life Application Bible.*

[8] Bible Note for Psalm 97:10, *Nelson's New King James Version* (Nashville, TN: Thomas Nelson Publishers, 1997)

Chapter Ten

[1] Bible Note for Psalm 129:2, *Life Application Bible* (Iowa Falls, IA: World Bible Publishers, Inc., 1989).

[2] Beth Moore. *Stepping Up: A Journey through the Psalms of Ascent* (Nashville, TN: LifeWay, 2007), 110.

[3] Bible Note for Psalm 35:4, *The English Standard Version* (Wheaton, IL: Crossway, 2008).

[4] Bible Note for Psalm 129:5, *Nelson's New King James Version* (Nashville, TN: Thomas Nelson Publishers, 1997)

[5] Bible Note for Obadiah 1:12, *Life Application Bible.*

[6] Bible Note for Psalm 35:4, *The English Standard Version.*

Chapter Eleven

[1] Bible Note for Psalm 130:1, *Nelson's New King James Version* (Nashville, TN: Thomas Nelson Publishers, 1997)

[2] Bible Note for Psalm 130:2, *Life Application Bible* (Iowa Falls, IA: World Bible Publishers, Inc., 1989).

[3] Bible Note for Romans 6:23, *Life Application Bible.*

[4] Bible Note for 2 Chronicles 36:16, *Life Application Bible.*

[5] Bible Note for Micah 1, *Life Application Bible.*

[6] Walter C. Kaiser, Jr. *The Journey Isn't Over* (Grand Rapids, MI: Baker Book House, 1993), 118.

[7] Bible Note for Ephesians 5:6, *Life Application Bible.*

Chapter Twelve

[1] Jonathan Edwards, "Humility" http://www.goodreads.com/author/quotes/75887.Jonathan_Edwards (accessed 15 Jun. 2013).

[2] Bible Note for 1 Peter 5:5, *Life Application Bible* (Iowa Falls, IA: World Bible Publishers, Inc., 1989).

[3] Ibid.

[4] Bible Note for Psalm 66:18, *Life Application Bible.*

[5] Bible Note for 2 Chronicles 32:31, *Life Application Bible.*

[6] Bible Note for 2 Kings 20:12-19, *Life Application Bible.*

[7] Ibid.

[8] .Bible Note for Deuteronomy 29:29, *Life Application Bible.*

[9] Bible Note for Philippians 4:11, *Life Application Bible.*

Chapter Thirteen

[1] Bible Note for Psalm 132, *Life Application Bible* (Iowa Falls, IA: World Bible Publishers, Inc., 1989).

[2] Bible Note for Psalm 132:2, *Life Application Bible.*

[3] Beth Moore. *Stepping Up: A Journey through the Psalms of Ascent* (Nashville, TN: LifeWay, 2007), 140.

[4] Bible Note for 1 Corinthians 6:19, *Life Application Bible.*

[5] James Strong. LL.D., S.T.D. *The New Strong's Complete Dictionary of Bible Words* (Nashville, TN: Thomas Nelson Publishers, 1996), 541.

[6] Profile of Eli for Bible Note for 1 Samuel 2:29, *Life Application Bible.*

[7] Bible Note for 1 Samuel 2:31, *Life Application Bible.*

[8] Arthur Pink, "Honoring God," http://gracegems.org/Pink/honoring_god.htm (accessed 9 April 2013).

[9] Ezra's profile in Ezra 7, *Life Application Bible.*

[10] Bible Note for 1 Kings 11:36, *Nelson's New King James Version* (Nashville, TN: Thomas Nelson Publishers, 1997).

[11] http://www.gotq2uestions.org "What does the Bible Say About a Christian Serving in the Military," (accessed 6 June 2013).

Chapter Fourteen

[1] Dr. Dan Hayden, "Reproof," http://www.awordfromtheword.org/reproof (accessed 15 July 2013).

[2] Ibid.

[3] Ibid.

[4] Profile of Absalom, *Life Application Bible* (Iowa Falls, IA: World Bible Publishers, Inc., 1989).

[5] Charles R. Swindoll. *A Man of Passion and Destiny: David* (Dallas, TX: Word Publishing, 1997) 195

6 Bible Note for Ephesians 4:3, *Life Application Bible*

7 Angela Smith, "The Power of a Three-Stranded Cord in an Unequal
Marriage," http://www.spirituallyunequalmarriage.com/my_
weblog/2011/03/the-power-of-a-three-stranded-cord-in-an-unequal-
marriage (accessed 16 July 2013).

8 R. Tuck, "Fragrance of the Brotherhood," http://ibiblestudies.com/auth/
tuck/fragrance_of_the_brotherhood.htm (accessed 10 July 2013).

9 Eugene H. Peterson. *A Long Obedience in the Same Direction* (Downer
Grove, IL: Intervarsity Press, 2000), 182

10 Ibid.

11 Ibid.

12 Walter C. Kaiser, Jr. *The Journey Isn't Over* (Grand Rapids, MI.: Baker Book
House Company, 1993), 146.

13 Peterson, 182.

Chapter Fifteen

1 *Merriam-Webster's Collegiate Dictionary,* Eleventh Edition, s.v. (Springfield,
MA: Merriam-Webster, Inc., 2005).

2 Ibid.

3 "Psalm 134." http://www.biblestudytools.com/commentaries/treasury-of-
david/psalms-134-1.html (accessed 25 July 2013).

4 Ibid.

5 Bible Note for Psalms 134:1-3, *Life Application Bible*.

6 Walter C. Kaiser, Jr. *The Journey Isn't Over* (Grand Rapids, MI: Baker Book
House Company, 1993), 150.

7 Ibid.

8 "Psalm 134." http://www.biblestudytools.com/commentaries/treasury-of-
david/psalms-134-1.html (accessed 25 July 2013.

9 Bible Note for 1 Chronicles 9:33, 34, *Life Application Bible* (Iowa Falls, IA:,
World Bible Publishers, Inc., 1989).

10 Ibid.

11 Eugene H. Peterson. *A Long Obedience in the Same Direction* (Downers
Grove, IL:, InterVarsity Press, 2000) 193.

12 Kaiser, 150.

13 Bible Note for Psalm 134:1-3, *Life Application Bible*.

Printed in the USA
CPSIA information can be obtained
at www.ICGtesting.com
JSHW022340140824
68134JS00019B/1589

9 781614 489962